Community profiling

Auditing social needs

Murray Hawtin
Geraint Hughes
Janie Percy-Smith
with Anne Foreman

Open University Press
Buckingham · Philadelphia

Open University Press
Celtic Court
22 Ballmoor
Buckingham
MK18 1XW

email: enquiries@openup.co.uk
world wide web: http://www.openup.co.uk

and

325 Chestnut Street
Philadelphia, PA 19106, USA

First Published 1994
Reprinted 1994, 1995 (twice), 1996, 1998, 1999 (twice)

A catalogue record of this book is available from the British Library

ISBN 0 335 19113 4 (pbk)

Library of Congress Cataloging-in-Publication Data

Hawtin, Murray, 1953–
    Community profiling : auditing social needs / Murray Hawtin,
Geraint Hughes, and Janie Percy-Smith.
      p. cm.
    Includes bibliographical references and index.
    ISBN 0–335–19113–4 (pbk.)
    1. Social surveys. 2. Community—Research. I. Hughes, Geraint,
1966– . II. Percy-Smith, Janie. III. Title.
HN29.H38 1994   93-39909
307'.072—dc20   CIP

Typeset by Colset Private Limited, Singapore
Printed in Great Britain by St Edmundsbury Press Limited,
Bury St Edmunds, Suffolk

Contents

List of figures

Preface

In 1990, the Policy Research Unit, Leeds Metropolitan University, published a short pamphlet entitled *Finding Out About Your Community: How to do a Social Audit*. This was intended as a guide for community groups and community practitioners wanting to undertake their own social audits or community profiles. Unexpectedly, this pamphlet proved to be a Policy Research Unit 'best seller'. Since that time, the authors, together with other colleagues in the Policy Research Unit, have undertaken a number of other social audits and community profiles which have added to our practical knowledge. In addition, the ideas contained in the original pamphlet have been discussed, criticized and commented upon in a number of different fora.

The current book draws upon the original pamphlet, the experience we have gained in the field since writing it and our useful discussions with others working on similar community profiling and social auditing projects. It is intended as a practical guide for all those who are engaged in community profiling, social auditing, needs assessments or community consultations. This group might include community practitioners and community workers as well as community and voluntary groups interested in profiling their own communities. It is likely to be of interest to social science and other students who are required to undertake community-based research.

The book works on a 'need-to-know' basis. It is not a comprehensive review of social science research methods. There are plenty of other texts which provide this kind of information. However, it does provide a basic, step-by-step guide for those wishing to undertake a community profile or social audit. For those interested in following up particular aspects in more detail, the guides to further reading which appear at the end of each chapter should be of help. The annotated bibliography which appears at the end of the book provides some examples of different types of community profiles and social audits which have been undertaken by a variety of different organizations. This bibliography is not comprehensive and we would welcome additions to our database which readers might like to send us.

A book of this kind which draws on the practical experience gained over a number of years, while written by the authors who appear on the cover, constitutes a distillation of the knowledge, skills, expertise and experience of a much wider group of people. Although the book is the sole responsibility of the authors, we recognize with gratitude and appreciation the contributions of our colleagues at the Policy Research Unit and those of others elsewhere with whom we have discussed ideas over a number of years. In addition, we acknowledge with thanks the contributions of all those communities who have allowed us to profile them, assess their needs or do social auditing work in their midst. We hope that that practical research experience in and with communities is reflected in the style, tone and approach of this book.

1

What is a community profile?

Introduction

Community profiling as a tool of community development is not new – many people will remember the community self-surveys that were undertaken in the 1970s. Others will be aware of similar work undertaken in the USA and the Netherlands as early as the 1950s (see Chapter 3). During the 1980s and 1990s, a group of related techniques – community profiling, needs assessments, social audits and community consultations – have been enjoying a new lease of life. The 1980s saw the widespread use of the term 'social audit' to describe studies that sought to demonstrate the impact on communities of changes in public policy or of major factory closures.[1] At about the same time, the Archbishop of Canterbury's Report, *Faith in the City*, was published, which suggested that inner-city churches might undertake parish audits as a way of reassessing their role in urban communities.[2]

The 1990s have seen a series of central government initiatives which require assessments of local needs or community consultations to be carried out. These have included Community Care, City Challenge, Neighbourhood Renewal initiatives and Estate Action. In some cases, the government's intention in introducing such requirements has not been to encourage more open, participative styles of working on the part of health and local authorities. Rather, they can be seen as yet another aspect of the political attack on local authorities and the undermining of their role and functions. However, even if one does not agree with the motive and while there is no guarantee that such assessments of need or community consultations will adopt the kinds of participative, profiling techniques described in the following chapters, they could be carried out in this way to the benefit of all concerned.

At the same time, many local authorities, faced with a rising tide of poverty, disadvantage and inequality in their areas together with diminishing resources with which to address such problems, have used social audits or community profiles to inform decision making about the allocation of resources.[3] Some local authorities are also using community profiles to inform strategies for the development of decentralized and comprehensive service delivery.[4] Others have recognized their use in developing baselines which can then be used in the monitoring and evaluation of policies and programmes.[5] Increasingly, too, statutory agencies are interested in ways of obtaining feedback from their 'customers' reflecting the new emphasis on the needs of the customer as opposed to those of the producer.

Communities themselves have also initiated or carried out profiles as a way of demonstrating to statutory service providers that they are not receiving an adequate level of services or that they have needs that are not currently being met or to demonstrate opposition to initiatives that will adversely affect them.[6]

In this chapter, we shall review the range of exercises that go under the name of needs assessment, community consultation, social audit or community profile. We shall then go on to look at the different situations in which such techniques might be useful and possible applications.

Needs assessment, community consultation, social audit or community profile?

There are currently a range of different terms around to describe what may appear to be similar exercises – needs assessment, community consultation, social audit and community profile are perhaps the most common. Are they all describing the same kinds of things or do they signify different kinds of approach? While these terms are often used by different people in different ways, it is nevertheless possible to identify some distinguishing features which mark them out from each other. These distinctive features become apparent in the ways in which the following questions are answered:

- What is the purpose of the exercise?
- Who is initiating the project?
- To what extent is the community involved?
- What is the scope of the exercise?

Needs assessment

In general, needs assessments tend to be initiated and/or carried out by a statutory body, for example a health authority, for policy planning purposes. They tend to rely heavily on existing data that have already been collected and are fairly particular in their focus covering just one policy issue. The most obvious examples are the health needs assessments that health authorities are now required to carry out under the terms of the NHS and Community Care Act 1990. While it is possible and even desirable to involve the community in such needs assessments, this does not always occur.[7] Sometimes this is because the geographical or administrative area to be covered is too large for communities to be involved in any practical sense. Or it may be because the resources available for needs assessment exercises – including financial resources, time and expertise – are in short supply in the agencies concerned. Nevertheless, while needs assessments undertaken at the level of the wider administrative area may not include many opportunities for primary research (collecting new information) or community involvement, there have been a number of more local needs assessments undertaken by community practitioners wanting to develop services more attuned to the needs of people on their 'patch'.[8]

Community consultation

Increasingly, statutory bodies such as local authorities, health authorities and also more recently developed bodies such as Urban Development Corporations, Housing Action Trusts and City Challenge Boards, have to consult with the local community about their programmes. However, once again, many of these consultations are, in practice, perfunctory and may, as a result, engender cynicism on the part of those communities whose support is required for successful implementation of such policies and programmes. Of course, this is not necessarily the case and there are examples of genuine consultation with communities.[9] Community consultations are rather different from community profiles, social audits or needs assessments, in that they usually take place in relation to a set of proposals for action that have been developed by an agency. They can, however, also be seen as an ongoing part of community profiling, social auditing or needs assessment exercises which have, as one of their aims, the active involvement of the community. In this case, community consultation might be undertaken at a number of key points in the process (see Chapter 3).

Social audits

Social audits have been initiated or carried out by a wide variety of different organizations, both statutory services and voluntary or community organizations. Although they typically include an assessment of need, they tend to be wider in their scope than the type of needs assessment described above, covering many more aspects of social life. The term social audit encapsulates the relationship between needs on the one hand and resources on the other. Just as a financial audit can reveal the financial health of an organization through an official examination of its accounts, a social audit attempts to reveal the 'health' of a community which results from the interplay of public services, housing, employment, the natural and social environment and many other factors.

Social audits may be conducted at a community level[10] and involve the collection of new primary data about the perceptions of those living or working in that community, or at the city or district level where the focus tends to be more on identifying inequities between communities for the purpose of reallocating resources.[11] In such cases, the information used to compile the audit is more likely to be data that are already in existence, for example health statistics, housing benefit data, unemployment data and information on service provision derived from the service departments themselves.

Community profile

The term community profile is perhaps the broadest in that it is used to refer to a diverse range of projects undertaken or initiated by different organizations including communities themselves, statutory agencies and voluntary organizations. They also tend to be broadest in their scope covering both needs and resources and the whole range of issues affecting communities. What is perhaps distinctive about community profiles is the extent to which the community is involved. Whereas needs assessments and social audits may benefit from the active involvement of the community, in practice this does not always occur. However, a good community profile, in our view, does require active community involvement.

Because 'community profile' is the term which has the broadest application and because it is most likely to conform to certain principles of community development described in the next section, this is the term that we will generally use throughout this book except where approaches or techniques are discussed that relate particularly to needs assessment, community consultation or social audit.

A community profile might, then, be defined as follows:

> A *comprehensive* description of the *needs* of a population that is defined, or defines itself, as a *community*, and the *resources* that exist within that community, carried out with the *active involvement of the community* itself, for the purpose of developing an *action plan* or other means of improving the quality of life in the community.

Elements of a community profile

There are a number of elements of this definition which require explanation and justification. The first of these is the comprehensive nature of the description which constitutes a community profile. While we are not suggesting that all community profiles are, in practice, comprehensive, in our view a good community profile *ought* to be comprehensive. The totality of individuals' and communities' lives do not conform to departmental and agency boundaries. The difficulties which people experience in their everyday lives cannot be neatly defined as 'housing problems' or 'health' or 'social isolation'. Rather, difficulties often interact in such a way that the whole is greater than the sum of the constituent parts. Of course, social researchers and those charged with meeting social needs and providing services know about the relationships between, for example, poor housing and ill health or unemployment and depression. However, practice has often been slow in reflecting this reality. So policies designed to combat poor housing, ill health, unemployment and mental health problems are still often formulated and implemented in isolation from each other. Community profiles which are comprehensive in their coverage will challenge that bureaucratic departmentalism as well as more accurately reflecting the reality of people's lives.

The second element of the definition of a community profile which we draw attention to is 'needs and resources'. We deliberately include this as a pair, since it is vital that a community profile describes not only the needs of a community but also the resources that exist within the community. By *resources* we mean assets held in the area and put to use for the benefit of the community. These could include, for example, the housing stock, parks, hospitals and community centres as well as people's time and expertise made available to others, or the employment opportunities within a given area and their product, service or wealth-distributing function. In any community there are also under-utilized resources; it may be important to find out why they are under-utilized and how they can be utilized more effectively. There are also likely to be potential resources, for example derelict buildings or vacant land which, while they serve no useful purpose at the moment, could be put to the use of the community with appropriate changes.

When we talk about resources, however, we also mean those intangible resources that are a source of strength and potential within the community. These might include such things as the skills – both formal and informal – of members of the community, networks of support such as families, households and neighbours, resilience and determination. To focus solely on what is needy about a community can not only be disheartening, perhaps reinforcing a negative image which its members are seeking to change, it is likely not to be a true reflection of the community.

Resources are often seen simply in terms of money and this is of course an important resource for any community. Social audits in particular have been used to show how much money is used to run services in an area and to reveal whether one particular area or group has a just distribution of those resources in terms of the needs of its population.[12] Extra money is commonly seen as the only way of meeting so far unmet needs, but this may not always be the case. There might be different ways of utilizing existing resources or delivering existing services. A social audit may also point to new ways of employing local people in the delivery of local services and retaining resources within the area. The audit can also be a way of reviewing whether proposals for using resources have really met the needs for which they were intended.

It is now increasingly common to find references to individual and collective *needs* in community profiling and social auditing work as well as in needs assessments. However, the concept of need is still the subject of considerable debate. That debate has focused on whether there is such a thing as objective need, who should define what counts as need, how needs can be researched and how it is possible to choose between competing needs. No matter how these questions are answered, what is clear is that need is increasingly being seen as a legitimate basis on which to make decisions about the allocation of resources and service provision. As such, it is an important element in community profiles.[13]

In Chapter 3, we discuss what is meant by *community* at some length. At this point, it is enough to draw attention to some of the different ways of thinking about community. Perhaps the most common conception of community is that of a group of people who live or work in the same geographical location, for example a housing estate or neighbourhood. However, we might also want to define communities in terms of an administrative area such as a school catchment area, social services area or the area served by a particular health authority. Another way of thinking about a community is in the sense of a group of people with a shared or common interest arising out of certain common characteristics. For example, people working in the same industry might be assumed for certain purposes to share common interests even though they do not live in the same geographical area. Similarly, women, an ethnic minority group, children, people with disabilities might all be considered as communities of interest for certain purposes. However, this approach can also be problematic, since it may assign to a particular group a communality of interest that does not in reality exist. If we take the 'black' community as a case in point, then it may be true that black people as a group have a shared experience of white racism; however, this may obscure the many differences that exist within and between black communities. This may not necessarily invalidate the idea of talking about a particular community but should simply alert us to the possibility or even the likelihood of 'communities within communities'. It will then be important to identify both similarities and differences between those constituent communities.

A further element of the definition which deserves attention is that of *active community involvement*. Of course, it is possible to profile a community without the active involvement of that community. However, the description that results is likely to be different in certain significant respects from one which actively involves members of the community. To the extent that services provided to communities have failed adequately to address their needs, then part of the problem lies in an assumption on the part of service providers and policy makers that they know what the needs of a particular community are and how those needs might best be addressed. A good community profile should, in our view, include the active involvement of the community for the following reasons. It is likely to result in a fuller, more comprehensive and more accurate description of the community and hence form a better basis on which to make decisions about provision and the way forward. It is an important way in which a community can be empowered through the development of skills, confidence and awareness of issues relating to the community. Active involvement in a community-profiling exercise can also provide a focus for activity which might aid other aspects of community development. Chapter 3 offers some suggestions of ways of encouraging active involvement on the part of the community throughout the community-profiling process.

Finally, we include in our definition the idea of the community profile leading to an *action plan* or other means of improving the quality of life of the community. This is because it serves no useful purpose to produce information for its own sake. Recording a description of a community at one point in time just to add to the archives of the local history group will achieve very little besides a sense of time, energy and enthusiasm having been expended for no reason on the part of those who carried out the community profile. The aim of the community profile must be to improve the quality of life of members of that community. One way in which this goal might be achieved is through the development of an action plan which identifies issues, priorities and action to be taken, sets goals and targets and proposes a means of monitoring progress towards their achievement. We look at this issue in greater detail in the final chapter of the book.

What constitutes the description of the profiled community is likely to vary according to the purpose for which the profile is carried out and its aims and objectives. So, for example, the finished profile may take the form of a conventional written report or it might, alternatively, take the form of an exhibition, a video or a combination of these things. It is important that the medium selected to convey the information is appropriate to the audience it is aimed at, the purpose of the profile and the techniques used to gather the information (see Chapter 8). Which of these options one chooses must relate to the aims and objectives of the profiling project, the uses it is going to be put to and the resources available for the project. It is crucial that all the elements that go to make up the profile – who is to be involved in the profile, the type of information to be collected, the methods to be used to collect it and the values embodied in the process – should all reflect the aims, objectives and ultimate purposes of the community profile.

As important as the constituent elements of this definition of a community profile, and underpinning it, is adherence to a set of values. The best community profiles are those which not only efficiently and accurately collect, analyse and present information about the community, but which do so in a way that reflects adherence to, and practical implementation of, a set of values. The first of these is respect for the community to be profiled. The practical import of this is that, as far as possible, members of the community are involved in the profiling process in such a way that they gain something positive from that process beyond the information collected, that they do not feel as if the profile is something that is done to them. This might be a greater confidence in themselves as a community, the building of skills and capacities and a better sense of their own potential. It also means that members of the community must be listened to and their views incorporated at an early stage in the profiling process so that the design of the project reflects their concerns. At the fieldwork stage, it means that information is collected with sensitivity and confidentiality is respected. It also means that the process adheres to the basic principles of equality. The issue of how to go about involving the community in a profiling exercise is discussed in detail in Chapter 3.

Why profile communities' needs?

Let's move on to look at some of the reasons why organizations might be interested in profiling communities. Again we might usefully think of reasons in terms of the organizations which are initiating such work.

Statutory services

Increasingly, statutory services have a responsibility to assess needs in the areas for which they have responsibility (for example, as a result of the NHS and Community Care Act, the Children Act, etc.). In general, these kinds of needs assessments are of the type mentioned above, involving very little direct community participation, although there is no reason why this should necessarily be the case. The most imaginative and, we would argue, the most useful, use community-profiling techniques to get a full picture of the communities that are to be served.[14]

Some recent government policy initiatives such as City Challenge and Neighbourhood Renewal areas require consultations with the community and these can take the form of community-profiling exercises. For example, neighbourhood renewal assessments require an assessment of an area's housing, environment, community, commerce, industry and land; the finding out of the views of residents and other 'stakeholders', especially the private sector; the development, timetabling and cost–benefit analysis of options for neighbourhood renewal; and the selection, with consultation, of the best option as an action plan for the renewal area.

There is no reason why this should not conform to the principles of community profiles that we have described so far. However, in reality, many such exercises are undertaken half-heartedly and superficially because there is a requirement that they be carried out. Community-profiling exercises undertaken for cosmetic reasons – to be seen to have consulted – are likely to engender mistrust and cynicism on the part of the community and, indeed, jeopardize the successful implementation of the precise initiative that they were designed to facilitate.

Statutory services may also use community-profiling exercises to obtain accurate information that is of relevance to various stages of the policy process. For example, community profiling may assist in the process of identifying those communities in most need for the purposes of reallocating resources between areas or groups or to target resources more effectively.[15] This might form the first part of an anti-poverty or equality strategy. Such strategies often begin with a city or area-wide 'poverty profile' based on existing data in order to identify areas or, less commonly, groups, where disadvantage is especially prevalent.[16] This may then lead on to a more detailed profile of those areas or groups in order to identify more precisely the remedial action that is necessary.

Statutory agencies have also used community profiling as a means of identifying shortfalls in service delivery in an attempt to improve the quality of service delivery, for example by orienting services more towards the needs of user groups rather than those of producers, by familiarizing service providers with the communities they are serving or by ensuring better coordination of services between departments or agencies.[17] Again this kind of exercise frequently takes the form of a straightforward market research exercise designed to obtain customer views. However, the most imaginative adopt a broader, more holistic approach, starting with needs (rather than existing provision) and working out from there to discover what services the community really needs and how these might best be delivered. Community profiling can also be a useful means of evaluating policy outcomes to ensure that policies and programmes are effective.

In rural areas, parish councils have used community profiles or village appraisals as 'the first step taking a community down a development path whereby community assets are used to "plug the gaps" identified in village life by the appraisal exercise'.[18] Many of these appraisals have been carried out using a standard software programme called *Village Appraisals* (see Chapter 7).

Voluntary/community organizations

Voluntary or community organizations have used community-profiling exercises as a means of demonstrating to service providers that the community has needs that are not being met or that it lacks services or resources of a particular type.[19] Community profiles have also been used as the basis of campaigns against particular developments. Social audits, in particular, have been used to demonstrate the impact or effects of change on the quality of life of a community, notably the effects of closing factories, the opening of retail outlets and also in monitoring the effects of competitive tendering and other changes in government policy.[20] Communities have also used community-profiling exercises as part of campaigns for or against new developments affecting them.

Community profiles have been used by both statutory and community organizations as part of a broader community development strategy (see Chapter 9). If this is the primary reason for undertaking the community profile, the emphasis is likely to be as much on the process of generating community involvement and building the community's skills, capacities and confidence through the process of undertaking the profile, as on the information collected.[21] For a community profile to fulfil this community development function, then it must meet a number of criteria.[22]

First, the community must be involved at all stages of the exercise (design, fieldwork, analysis and follow-up) and hence achieve a sense of ownership of both the process and the outcomes. This means that sufficient time must be allowed for preparation and initial groundwork and the subsequent work must also take place at a pace appropriate to the community. Second, the community-profiling process must be designed in ways that generate ideas and discussion and lead to action. Third, it is especially important in a community development context that mechanisms are built into the process for communication about what is happening both during and after the profile. Fourth, the profiling process should go beyond an assessment of needs and become a positive exercise identifying strengths and opportunities within communities. And, finally, the community profile should, where possible, provide opportunities for a variety of views to be expressed across a wide range of subjects and to make connections between issues.

Community profiles might also be used by voluntary or community groups as a way of holding policy makers and politicians more accountable. The community profile can establish a baseline or bench mark against which the effectiveness of subsequent developments may be measured.[23] They might also be used as a means of community or voluntary groups reassessing the relevance of their activities. We have already mentioned the parish audits which have been widely conducted following the publication of *Faith in the City*, as a means of inner-city churches reviewing the appropriateness of their activities.[24]

Of course, there may be more than one reason for undertaking a single community profile. However, in such cases, it is important that the aims and objectives of the project are drawn up precisely and that the various reasons for undertaking the profile are not in conflict with each other. Similarly, it is important that each reason does not engender its own profiling exercise, which will simply generate survey fatigue on the part of everyone concerned, most especially the community.

Key issues

Needs assessments, social audits, community consultations and community profiles, while they share certain features in common, can be distinguished from each other in terms of the agencies which are typically involved, the purpose of the exercise, the extent of community involvement and the scope of the exercise. Community profiling is probably the broadest of these terms and is the main focus of this book. A community profile can be defined as:

> A comprehensive description of the needs of a population that is defined, or defines itself, as a community, and the resources that exist within that community, carried out with the active involvement of the community itself, for the purpose of developing an action plan or other means of improving the quality of life of the community.

The key words in this definition are 'comprehensive', 'needs', 'resources', 'community', 'active involvement' and 'action plan'.

There are a number of reasons why agencies might wish to undertake community-profiling work. Statutory agencies may be required to assess local needs; they may use community profiles as a means of obtaining accurate information of relevance to policy planning, implementation, monitoring and evaluation. Alternatively, voluntary or community organizations may initiate a community-profiling exercise as a means of demonstrating the existence of unmet needs or inadequate resources or as part of a community campaign for or against a particular development. They may also use community profiles as a means of providing baseline information to be used as a benchmark for assessing future developments. Community profiles, provided they conform to certain criteria, may also be used as part of a community development strategy. In such cases, the process of doing the profile may be as important as the information collected.

Further reading

Department of Health (1993) *Population Needs Assessment: Good Practice Guide*. London: HMSO.

Doyal, L. and Gough, I. (1991) *A Theory of Human Need*. London: Macmillan.

Geddes, M. (1988) *Social Audits and Social Accounting: An Annotated Bibliography and Commentary*. London: South Bank Polytechnic.

Percy-Smith, J. (1992) 'Auditing social needs', *Policy and Politics*, Vol. 20, No. 1, pp. 29–34.

Notes

1. See, for example, *The Closure of Smurfit Corrugated Cases Ltd* (Merseyside County Council 1983); *Newcastle Upon Tyne – A Social Audit* (Newcastle City Council 1985).
2. Archbishop of Canterbury's Commission on Urban Priority Areas (1985) *Faith in the City: A Call for Action by Church and Nation.* London: Church House.
3. See, for example, *The Liverpool Quality of Life Survey* (Liverpool City Council 1989); London Research Centre (1991) *Needs in London: A Review of the Impact of Social Trends, Policy and Legislation 1990/91.* London: London Borough Grants Committee.
4. See, for example, *Mid Craigie and Linlathen Area Needs Assessment* (Tayside Regional Council 1987).
5. See Percy-Smith, J. (1992) 'Auditing social needs', *Policy and Politics*, Vol. 20, No. 1, pp. 29–34.
6. See, for example, Queenspark (1987) *Brighton on the Rocks.* Brighton: Queenspark Books.
7. See, however, Department of Health (1993) *Population Needs Assessment: Good Practice Guidance.* London: HMSO.
8. See, for example, Kirkstall Clinic (n.d.) *Community Profile of Kirkstall and Hawksworth.* Leeds: Kirkstall Clinic.
9. See, for example, Kneen, P. (1991) *Ragworth Neighbourhood Centre Consultation.* Middlesbrough: Cleveland County Council.
10. See, for example, *Loftus Community Action Area* (Cleveland County Council 1989).
11. See, for example, *Fair Shares? The Southwark Poverty Profile* (London Borough of Southwark 1987).
12. See, for example, *Newcastle Upon Tyne – A Social Audit* (Newcastle City Council 1985).
13. See, for example, Doyal, L. and Gough, I. (1991) *A Theory of Human Need.* London: Macmillan.
14. See, for example, Percy-Smith, J. and Sanderson, I. (1992) *Understanding Local Needs.* London: Institute for Public Policy Research; *Areas of Family Stress* (Cheshire County Council 1988).
15. See, for example, *Asian Survey: Education, Housing, Health and Community Provision* (Cleveland County Council 1982).
16. See, for example, *Central Newham Social Audit* (Newham Borough Council 1985).
17. See, for example, *Knottingley Profile* (City of Wakefield MDC 1989).
18. See *A Step by Step Guide to Conducting a Village Appraisal* (Community Council for Suffolk n.d.); see also *A Village Appraisal: Down Ampney, Gloucestershire* (Down Ampney Village Appraisal Group 1991).

19. See, for example, *Bloomsbury Safety Audit Phase One* (Safe Estates for Women 1992).
20. See, for example, *St John's Colliery Maesteg* (St John's NUM and Communities Action Committee 1985).
21. See, for example, *City Challenge Health Project* (City Challenge Health Project 1992).
22. Smith, J. (1993) Presentation to the *Issues in Community Profiling Seminar*, Policy Research Unit, Leeds, June.
23. Op. cit., note 5.
24. See, for example, Shiner, P. (1991) *The Cry of the People of Buttershaw*. Leeds: CANA; Browne, L. (1989) *Church and the Community*. Leeds: Policy Research Unit.

2

Planning a community profile

Having decided to do a community profile, the first step must be to plan the work. This is a vital part of the process itself and failure to spend sufficient time on it is likely to lead to difficulties later. This chapter takes you through the steps that you ideally need to include in your plan as shown in Fig. 2.1, and discusses in detail the issues and options associated with the first three stages of community profiling, which we have called 'Preparing the Ground', 'Setting Aims and Objectives' and 'Deciding on Methods'. These three stages are the planning and decision-making elements of the profiling process and, for that reason, are discussed in detail in this chapter. The stages of the profiling process concerned with information gathering, data analysis, presentation of findings and action planning are discussed in detail in subsequent chapters.

Preparing the ground

At the very beginning of a project, you will probably have a plan to do a profile of a particular community, a few interested people and some preliminary ideas about issues that you want to examine. In order to take the profile forward from the ideas stage to the practical work stage, there are a number of different tasks that will need to be accomplished. They are all important, since they will, in large part, set the tone for your future work, its scope and your style of working. The order in which these tasks are undertaken is less important than that they should all be accomplished.

Creating a steering group

One of the very first tasks that you need to undertake is to get additional people involved through the setting up of a project steering group. How much work you have to do in order to develop a

Figure 2.1   Stages in the community-profiling process

- **Preparing the ground**
  Creating a steering group
  Initial planning
  Making contacts
  Learning from others' experiences
  Identifying resources
  Engaging consultants or professional researchers
  Developing a management structure

- **Setting aims and objectives**

- **Deciding on methods**

- **Fieldwork**
  Production of information-gathering tools, e.g. questionnaires
  Training of staff involved in data collection
  Collecting 'new' information
  Recording information
  Analyzing information

- **Reporting**
  Writing up fieldwork
  Production of draft profile
  Consultations on draft profile
  Amendments to draft profile
  Production of final community profile
  Dissemination of research findings

- **Action**
  Consultations over key issues, priorities, action to be taken
  Drafting community action plan
  Consultations over draft plan
  Production of action plan
  Dissemination of action plan
  Implementation
  Monitoring and evaluation

project steering group may depend on how the idea to do a community profile came about. It may be the case that you already have a dedicated group of people who are committed to the idea. If not, then you will have to create such a group of people who will direct and organize the early stages of the work until such time as decisions are taken about how the project is to be managed. The ideal size for a steering group will vary considerably between projects and will depend on the size of the community, the scope of the profile to be undertaken and the time and dedication of those involved. It might be as small as two or three committed and energetic people or as large as twelve or thirteen. Whatever the number, the group must be small enough to work effectively but large enough that interested people are not excluded. Chapter 3 includes some additional ideas about involving the community in this stage of the project.

There are a number of ways in which you might go about assembling a group of people to form a steering group. The aim is to recruit people who share a commitment to the idea but who come from a variety of different organizations (even if the project is led, by necessity, by one agency) or who are likely to offer a range of different perspectives so that the project is not dominated from the outset by a particular viewpoint. One way to do this is to organize a public meeting in an appropriate venue which is widely publicized and indicate that all are welcome to come. The problem with this approach is that you have no idea at all who, if anyone, will turn up and whether they have any real understanding of what you are trying to achieve.

It might be better, at this stage, to write a letter setting out what you want to do and why and send it to as many groups and individuals in the community in which you are interested inviting them to come to a meeting. Some of the groups and organizations you might wish to contact are listed in Fig. 2.2. Of course, the kinds of groups who you get in touch with will vary according to whether you are profiling a geographical community or a group of people sharing common characteristics. If you are doing the former, then you will want to invite representatives from the statutory services who work in that community; if you are doing the latter, you may wish to invite a person who has special responsibility for developing or providing services for that particular group. For example, if you are profiling women in your city, then you may want to invite local authority departments to send an officer who has special responsibility for services for women and any group or organization that campaigns on women's issues.

In addition, you may want to invite representatives of groups who have resources of various kinds which you may wish to make use of, such as your local Council for Voluntary Services, which may be a useful starting point for building up contacts, or anyone

Figure 2.2   Individuals, groups and organizations to invite to the initial steering group meeting

---

- **Statutory services**
  Social Services
  Housing
  Police
  Library
  Leisure/sports centre
  Local schools
  Planning department
  Health centre
  Youth services
  Headteacher

- **Voluntary/community organizations**
  Tenants/residents group
  Neighbourhood association
  Elderly persons luncheon club
  Parent and toddler group
  Campaigning groups, e.g. Age Concern, Gingerbread, Mencap, etc.

- **Community representatives**
  Ward councillors (parish, district/city, county)
  MP
  MEP
  Other community 'leaders'

---

with an interest in community development or social science research methods at your local university.

In general, you are more likely to get a positive response if you can send your invitation to a named individual rather than to the organization. If it has gone to the 'wrong' person, then they are quite likely to pass it on to a more appropriate person. When you write to these individuals, groups and organizations, it is a good idea to include a tear-off slip asking people to indicate whether they are attending and, if not, whether they would like to be kept informed of progress.

At the meeting, you will need to set out clearly what it is you are trying to do and why and explain the purpose of the meeting. By the end of the meeting, you should be have achieved all the objectives listed in Fig. 2.3.

Figure 2.3 Objectives of initial steering group meeting

- Reach a shared understanding of what, in broad terms, the project is about
- Gain a view about the extent to which people think it is a good idea. (If not many people are in favour, you may need to go away and think again!)
- Obtain a commitment from a group of those present to constitute themselves as a steering group
- Agree the terms of reference of the steering group
- Identify the next steps that need to be taken
- Agree a time and place for the next meeting

This is more than enough to do at the first meeting! However, try to arrange the next meeting for a date fairly soon after, as you still have a lot of work to do before the steering group can really function effectively. At the next meeting, you may find yourself concentrating on the group itself and how it should work. There are a number of issues which need to be addressed, as shown in Fig. 2.4. This may be a time-consuming discussion, but it is especially important if the steering group is also to be the project management group. If, however, the steering group intends to hand over to a different project management group at a later date, then you may feel that some of these issues are best left until later. Having addressed these issues, the group is then in a position to move on to the more substantive issues of relevance to the profile.

Figure 2.4 The organization of the steering group

- Is the steering group as it is presently constituted an appropriate size?
- Are there other people who you need to get on board at this stage?
- How often will the group meet?
- Who will be responsible for convening meetings?
- Will there be an agenda and minutes? If so, who is responsible for drawing them up?
- Who is allowed to have access to these documents?
- Is there to be a chairperson? If not, how will meetings be organized/coordinated?

There are six tasks that need to be accomplished quite quickly. These are: initial planning, including preliminary identification of the community and issues to be covered by the profile; making contact with relevant community groups, leaders, key actors; learning from others' experience; identifying available resources; engaging consultants or professional researchers; and the development of a management structure. We shall look in turn at what each of these entails. You might want to assign responsibility for the completion of these tasks to different members of the steering group, so that the burden of work is shared and also to maintain commitment and enthusiasm on the part of group members.

Initial planning

At this point in the process, you will have an effectively functioning group with an idea or several ideas. The next task is to refine those ideas into something workable. The first important decision that you have to make is what exactly is the community that is going to be profiled. If you are interested in a geographically located community, then it is useful to start off with a street map of the whole area. Begin by marking any 'natural' boundaries to the community such as a park, railway line or motorway. This may identify some boundaries but is unlikely to identify all of them. There are at least three other relevant considerations which may help you define your community. The first is commonly held local views about where the community or neighbourhood begins or ends. The second is whether there are any administrative boundaries that cut across your area. It is always easier to work with data that relate to the boundaries you are working with. The most obvious administrative boundaries which you may want to draw in on your map are Census Enumeration Districts (EDs), Polling Districts and statutory service administrative boundaries such as health, housing and social services. In practice, these rarely coincide with each other, but it is important to at least know where they are. The final consideration is to define your community in such a way that it is manageable in terms of size.

If, on the other hand, your chosen community is a 'community of interest', for example women, an ethnic group or young people, you may still have to make decisions about boundaries. For example: Are you going to include women from throughout the district or city or just one part of the city? What age groups are you going to include in the category 'young people'? Exactly which ethnic group are you interested in? A further consideration is how you intend to identify your community. (There is further information on this in the section on 'Samples and sampling' in Chapter 6.)

A further task to be accomplished as part of this initial planning is to identify a preliminary list of issues that you want to examine as part of the community profile. For example, is your profile intended to be comprehensive, covering most issues that affect people such as health, housing, the environment, employment, welfare services, education, child care, transport and so on? Or are you focusing on a more limited range of issues such as skills, training and employment, or needs and resources in relation to welfare provision? At this stage, you should regard this list of issues as provisional pending consultations with a wider group.

Making contacts

Now you are in a position to begin to develop contacts within the community that you have identified and begin some initial consultation about the scope of the profile. You should already have begun to compile a list of key individuals and organizations within your community and the steering group should now begin to add to this. Having got as complete a list as possible, you then need to inform them about the project, seek their support and cooperation, and arrange to talk to as many people as possible. The first step in this process is likely to be the sending out of a letter giving details of the project, inviting comments and/or suggesting that the letter will be followed up within a week or so with a telephone call to arrange a meeting to discuss the project further. You may not have the resources or the time to see all these groups and individuals at this stage; if not, make sure that you have at least contacted the people who you think are the most important community 'gatekeepers' (e.g. representatives of ethnic minority community associations in areas where the ethnic minority population is significant) and a cross-section of others, for example some representatives of voluntary, community and statutory organizations, some elected community representatives and so on. If you do have to prioritize who to see, then be aware of the politics of your community. There may be groups or individuals who will take offence if they are not consulted at this early stage.

Rather than talking only to representatives or leaders of groups (who may not be truly representative), it might be a better idea to contact groups like mother and toddler groups, tenant associations and so on, and ask if you can have a half-hour 'slot' at some point during their next meeting to explain the project, invite questions, comments, suggestions and offers of help. One of the aims of this series of meetings is to add to and amend your initial list of issues and to identify 'resources' (see below).

Learning from others' experience

A further task that can be usefully carried out at this stage is to find out whether anyone else has tried to do something similar to what you are planning to do and whether there are any other major pieces of community development work planned for your area. To help in tracking down groups and organizations which have engaged in social auditing or community profiling work, we have compiled an annotated bibliography which, although it is undoubtedly incomplete, may provide you with some initial leads. In addition, Councils for Voluntary Services often have copies of profiles relating to their area and Citizens Advice Bureau workers, health visitors and community nurses sometimes have to draw up a local profile as part of their training. Talking to other people who have undertaken a similar exercise to your own before you start work can enable you to learn from their experience and, hopefully, avoid any mistakes which they may have made.

Identifying resources

Any community-profiling exercise relies for its success on having a quite extensive range of resources. It is very important to have a clear understanding of three issues in relation to resources: What resources do the group already have or have access to? What resources do the group need but do not have at the moment? Which of these are vital for the successful completion of the project and how can they be obtained? You might want to draw up a grid along the lines indicated in Fig. 2.5 to help with this process.

Some external sources of assistance which you may want to consider using are staff from (1) your local university or college of further education, who may be able to offer help with survey design and data analysis; (2) a community resource centre, who may be able to provide assistance with printing and photocopying; (3) your local Planning Department, who may be willing to supply

Figure 2.5 Resources grid

Resource	Available in group	Vital	Can be obtained from
Person power			
Money			
Design skills			
Computing skills			
Interviewing skills			
Group work skills			
Computer			
Photocopier			
Access to information			
Maps			
Local contacts			

maps free of charge; (4) a friendly, local librarian, who will help you track down documents relating to your community.

Engaging consultants or professional researchers

Depending on the financial resources which you have available and the expertise that you have within your group, you may want to engage consultants or professional researchers to undertake all or part of the work for you. Since this book is aimed principally at those intending to carry out most of the work themselves, we do not discuss this in detail. Again your local Council for Voluntary Services may be able to help you find an appropriate organization to assist you. However, it is worth saying that engaging professional researchers or consultants will itself entail considerable work. You will have to draw up a project specification setting out what the project is about, what you require the consultants to do, any ideas you have about the methods to be used or the style of working you would prefer, the contractual arrangements and how they should 'bid' for the work if you are approaching more than one organization. Having appointed researchers you will then have to write a contract specifying in detail the work to be done, the time-scale, the amount to be paid and when and how they are to report to you. In addition, you will have to work out a means of managing the consultants so that you have the amount of input into the work that you want, for example over the design of questionnaires or the wording of press releases. It can be very disappointing to spend a large amount of money on a piece of work carried out by professional researchers or consultants only to discover that they have not really done what you wanted them to do or they are not working in the way that you had expected. An alternative is to pay a professional researcher or consultant for, say, a day's worth of advice on questionnaire design or data analysis.

Development of a management structure

At some point during this initial, 'preparing-the-ground' stage, you will have to make a decision about how the project should be managed. It may be appropriate for the steering group to simply continue as the project management group. This is probably satisfactory if you are confident that the steering group contains a cross-section of representatives of the community and, more importantly, has credibility with that community. If this is not the case, then you will probably need to create a new management group to take the project forward. If the management group is going to have credibility with the community, then its appointment will have to occur at a public meeting which all members of, and stakeholders in, the community are invited to attend. You might also want to use this meeting to formally launch the community-profiling project with appropriate publicity. The meeting should be advertised widely using all or some of the following methods: posters and/or leaflets displayed in library, health centre, social services office, housing office, community centre, leisure centre, etc.; letters sent to community groups, voluntary organizations, community representatives and leaders inviting them to attend; press release sent to local newspapers; item included in 'open space' slot in local radio or television programme.

Having brought people together in this way, the steering group should explain to those attending what the project is about, what progress has been made to date and what the meeting is for. The main purpose of the meeting is to seek cooperation and support and elect, nominate or appoint a management committee. Whatever method you choose, you should bear in mind the fact that some people may be reluctant to put themselves forward, so you may need to encourage people to nominate others and possibly leave yourselves the option of co-opting people if you think that you have not got enough nominations or those that are being put forward are not drawn from a wide enough cross-section of the community.

In inviting nominations you need to make it clear what being a member of the management committee will entail in terms of the timing and frequency of meetings, other work that might be expected of them and so on. In addition, you need to consider the kinds of things that act as barriers to people who might like to be involved and how these might be overcome. The issues that you might consider include: the accessibility of the venue for meetings; the times when meetings are held; child care; and whether the way in which meetings are structured, organized and conducted is off-putting. However, it is also important that if the group promises to address particular barriers to participation that they can deliver on the promise; in other words, if there is a commitment to provide assistance with childcare or baby-sitting, that there are appropriate resources available to back that commitment.

Another consideration in constructing the management com-mittee is the size of the group. What is an appropriate size will depend in part on what you want the management committee to do. The committee needs to be large enough to provide sufficient people to undertake the work that has to be done but small enough to act as an effective decision-making body. In general, it is better to involve as many people who want to be involved as it is likely to cause bad feeling if some members of the community are excluded having put themselves forward, and anyway, some people will drop out over the course of the project.

Once a management committee has been appointed and some preliminary issues relating to timing and venues for meetings have been addressed, another meeting needs to be arranged quite quickly to which someone needs to bring a short draft paper setting out the terms of reference for the committee. These terms of reference should address the following issues:

- the membership of the management committee and whether this is fixed or open;
- the aims of the committee; and
- how committee meetings are to be organized and any rules of working.

The management committee should now be in a position to take over the running of the project from the steering group and it must now address the crucial question of what the aims and objectives of the project are going to be.

Setting aims and objectives

The aims and objectives of the community-profiling project will depend in large part on the overall purpose for which the profile is being carried out. In most cases, the profile will not be an end in itself but a means to an end. Figure 2.6 gives some examples of project aims and objectives for other community profiling exercises.

The aims and objectives that the group decides on must be clearly stated, quite specific and must be agreed to by the whole management group. It is important that the reason for doing the profile is kept in mind so that others do not attach their own objectives to the project making it too unwieldy. It may be that the list of objectives that is produced is too long to be manageable. If this is the case, then you will need to decide on priorities. Again keeping the overall purpose in mind will help to focus on what the priorities ought to be.

Deciding on methods

Having arrived at a set of aims and objectives, it should now be possible to decide on the methods to be used to undertake the profile. For each objective it should be possible to specify methods for the achievement of that objective. Essentially, the community profile is about information, so the objectives should relate to the kinds of information required and the methods through which that information is going to be collected. As a first step in deciding on methods, you may need to find out what information already exists that relates to the community in which you are interested. No matter what the precise focus of your profile, there is likely to be some information somewhere that is of relevance. It is worth assembling this or, at the very least, finding out what already exists before you start, so that you don't waste time and energy collecting information that someone else has already gathered. Chapter 4 suggests ways of going about this and offers ideas about possible sources.

You then need to go on to decide what additional information is needed to meet your objectives and begin to consider the ways

Figure 2.6 Examples of project aims and objectives

- To produce a community profile of South Seacroft including:
  - questionnaire and quantitative information on the economic, social and demographic character of the area
  - identification of individual and community needs
- To assess the impact on South Seacroft of targetted resources over the past year in the light of identified community needs with special reference to housing, health, and adult education and training [Brady, S. and Hughes, G. (1991) *Seacroft Sounds Out: A Community Profile* Leeds: Policy Research Unit]

- To ascertain the level of facilities within villages
- To see how these have changed since the earlier surveys
- To identify any gaps in the provision of services
  [*Village Facilities Survey, 1990* (Colchester Borough Council 1992)]

- Identify the social, economic and environmental factors and activities which characterize the estate
- Identify obstacles to employment of estate residents and ways to overcome these
- Consider ways in which the quality and efficiency of the delivery of public sector resources could be improved by careful coordination and avoidance of duplication of effort
- Through liaison with the private and public sectors, explore the potential for job creation, enterprise and training initiatives within the wider economic development area, which could benefit estate residents
- Formulate proposals which will act as a catalyst for change and bring about sustainable social, economic and environmental regeneration
  [Meadowell Initiative (1991) *A Strategy for Change*]

in which that information could be collected. Chapters 5 and 6 review in some detail the options that are open to you and you may need a quick look at these chapters at this stage so that you are in a better position to make decisions about methods.

Having decided what you want to do and how you want to do it, you need to cost what you want to do in terms of financial and other resources to see whether it is achievable. The resources that you need to complete the profile should then be compared with the initial list of resources that you drew up at the beginning of the project. With any luck that initial list can be added to now to include the additional people who have since become involved, together with the skills and knowledge that they bring. Once again your review should identify those resources which the group does not have at its disposal but which are vital for the successful completion of the project. If this list is too long, you may need to go back to the methods you have specified and think again about those which are especially resource-intensive.

At the same time that you are considering the methods to be used in the project, you will also need to consider the time-scale for the project and any externally imposed time constraints such as deadlines for the submission of funding applications, local authority committee cycles and so on. The timetable should reflect what you are going to do, the resources available to you and how long you think it will take to build up relationships with people in the community. Don't forget to allow for holidays that might interrupt work on the project. In general, you need to allow sufficient time to enable the work to be done properly but without dragging the process out over such a long period of time that people lose interest. In most cases, you will need between four and six months to do a profile from start to finish, although this will vary according to the particular circumstances of your project. In planning a timetable it is useful to start by listing each of the separate tasks that need to be completed and to identify which of them have to be completed in order for the next stage to begin and which can run alongside each other. You should then be able to divide the project up into stages and to set deadlines for the completion of each stage.

This is the end of the planning stage of the profile. By now you should be able to 'tick' all the items listed in Fig. 2.7.

Now you are ready to begin the process of collecting the new information that you need in order to complete your profile. This is a good time to put out some further publicity about the project, so that the community knows what has been achieved to date and what is going to happen next. This is especially important if you are going to do any survey work which will rely on the cooperation of individuals and groups. The remaining stages of the project are described in detail in subsequent chapters, so it is not necessary to do more than identify these stages from Fig. 2.1 so that they can be included in your planning and timetable.

Figure 2.7 Checklist of things to be achieved by the end of the 'preparing-the-ground' stage

---

- A *management committee* with clear terms of reference, roles and responsibilities
- Consensus about the *purpose* for doing the community profile
- Consensus about the *community* to be profiled
- A preliminary list of *issues* to be addressed by the profile
- A clearly stated set of *aims and objectives*
- A set of practicable *methods* for the achievement of these aims and objectives
- *Resources* that are appropriate to the task in hand
- *Contacts* within the community to be profiled
- Any *existing data* that relate to your community

Key issues

Spending time planning your community profile may seem to be time wasted that could be usefully spent getting on with the job. While it is important not to get too bogged down in planning at the expense of action, taking some time at the beginning of a project to think carefully and creatively about what you are trying to achieve and building up contacts and cooperation with the community is time well spent and could save time later. Many research projects ultimately fail either to be completed or to achieve their objectives because insufficient time was spent at the planning stage.

This chapter has focused on moving from an idea to do a community profile in the minds of a few individuals, through the creation of a small project steering group, to the setting up of a management committee. It has also taken the reader through the process of identifying preliminary issues, formulating aims and objectives, deciding on methods, mobilizing resources and planning a timetable. Work can now begin on collecting new information that will form the basis of the profile. The next two chapters will pick up two tasks mentioned in this chapter but not elaborated on – how to involve the community and how to collect and make use of existing information – before looking in detail at how to go about collecting, storing and analysing new information in Chapters 5–7.

Further reading

Bell, J. (1993) *Doing Your Research Project* 2nd edn. Buckingham: Open University Press.

Burton, P. (1993) *Community Profiling: A Guide to Identifying Local Needs*. Bristol: School of Advanced Urban Studies, University of Bristol.

Community Council for Suffolk (n.d) *A Step by Step Guide to Conducting a Village Appraisal*. Ipswich: Community Council for Suffolk.

Kane, E. (1991) *Doing Your Own Research*, Chs 1–3. London: Marion Boyars.

UPA Committee (n.d.) *Parish Audit Guidelines*. Manchester: UPA Committee, Manchester Diocese.

3

Involving the community

Introduction

It is possible to produce a community profile without the active
involvement of the community. However, involving members of a
community is likely to result in a more accurate and complete
description. It can also be argued that members of a community
have a right to be heard and to know what is being said about
them. But what exactly do we mean by *the community*? In this
chapter, we start by looking at this over-used, often hackneyed,
concept. Who constitutes the community? What lessons are there
to be learned from those who work specifically with communities?

Chapter 9 explores some of the ways in which community profiles can be used to assist in the process of empowering communities, and as part of a community development strategy. If these
are included in your profile's objectives, you will almost certainly
want to involve the community at every opportunity. In this
chapter, we look at the various levels of community involvement,
both in terms of the relative involvement of community members
on the one hand, and professionals or external helpers on the other,
and also in terms of the amount of involvement individuals might
have in the profiling process.

That process, as is shown in Fig. 2.1, comprises a number of
stages from the initial idea to undertake a profile through to using
the findings. You can – and we would argue should – involve
the community in all those stages directly or indirectly, and
that involvement will enhance the project. Communities may
not always welcome involvement in exercises of this kind and
encouraging full involvement is not always easy. We therefore
include practical suggestions for maximizing community involvement, both by encouraging active support and by removing some
of the barriers that prevent people from becoming more involved.

What is this thing called 'the community'?

A common bond

Before we can consider the theme of involving the community, it is essential to understand what we mean by the term 'community'. It is a word that is now very difficult to define precisely; its usage has become so pervasive in our everyday language that its meaning is overlaid with a host of associations (European Community, community chest, community policing), and also emotions (community charge, caring community, community spirit). Typically the word community is used to refer to the idea that there is something that is common to a group or section of the population. Communities may be based on *geographical areas or localities* ranging in size from a single street through estates, neighbourhoods, wards, other smaller administrative areas such as school catchment areas and parishes, villages, towns, districts, counties to nations and even groups of nations.

However, there are other characteristics besides geography or location which can form the basis of a community. These might include such things as age, gender, ethnicity or nationality. There are also other common bonds that can create the sense of belonging to a community, for example having a shared problem such as a medical condition or disability (visually impaired community), a shared working environment (miners' community), or membership of a religious or political organization (Catholic community). These definitions are not, of course, mutually exclusive, and it is possible to undertake a profile using several of these characteristics.[1]

In undertaking a community profile, you may also want to take account of the views of people who, while they are not by definition members of the community, nevertheless occupy positions which impact on the community. So, for example, a spatially defined community profile might include the views of those who represent the community in some way such as politicians (councillors, MPs and Euro-MPs) and also members of trusts and boards such as Housing Action Trusts, Urban Development Committees and School Government Boards.

Another category of people who may be seen to be part of a community are those who work in the community but do not necessarily live as part of it. This group would include those whose place of work just happens to be in the locality, those who work for the community (doctors, teachers, street cleaners, and so on) and those who not only work for the community but are also more directly accountable to it (such as community workers, patch social workers and community architects).

Conflicting communities

The term 'community' is usually seen in a positive light and may evoke feelings of closeness or warmth. However, not all communities conform to this picture. Although there are, no doubt, still communities like this, in many cases real efforts have to be made to develop a 'community spirit'. In reality, communities are not always comfortable, homogeneous entities. They are cross-cut by a variety of divisions – race, gender and class – and contain a multitude of groups whose interests may conflict with each other. In the most divided communities, these conflicts may be played out violently or through such behaviour as racial harassment.

It is therefore important to identify clearly any overt or underlying conflicting interests within a community. You should try and ensure that the views of all factions are heard and that representatives of all sections of the community have an equal opportunity to take part in the process. Failure to do so will not only produce an incomplete picture of the community but could also antagonize the under-represented section and exacerbate divisions.

Approaches to community involvement

'Professional' approach to community involvement

Many professional people who work in well-defined communities are resentful of colleagues' use of the term 'community' in their job title. Architects are often heard to say that they build in the community and so are all 'community architects'. However, there are often subtle differences between professional approaches to involvement in the community.

This divergence can be illustrated by Haggstrom's concept of communities that helped to inform the development of community work in the 1970s. His premise was that communities have two guises – community as *object* and *acting community*.[2] The first can be seen as a network of interdependent systems, bureaucratic organizations, interest groups, political parties and so on that is

Figure 3.1 Community work approach

> The organisation and structure of society cause problems of
> powerlessness, alienation and inequality. To achieve greater equality
> and social justice, resource and power must be redistributed.[2]

acted upon. Acting communities, on the other hand, identify their
own needs and problems, participate in decision making and
engage in collective action.

Many professionals will 'act on' communities, often in an expert
capacity, in the belief that it is in the communities' best interest.
However, they may unwittingly behave in a patronizing way,
creating dependency and the very state of community apathy that
so many of them deplore. A 'community work approach', however,
evolved in the 1960s and early 1970s that incorporated certain
beliefs and values (see Fig. 3.1). This approach does not see community involvement as just a means to another end (such as
providing a pleasant built environment) but as an end in itself (that
is empowerment). It incorporates the belief that 'acting communities' can lead to liberation, development and fulfilment through
cooperation, shared interests and values.

Community profiling and empowering the community

In order to fulfil the community development task and assist a
community to evolve from a passive recipient of services and goods,
to an active one where residents become empowered to take part
in a creative, liberating experience, it may be necessary to enable
that community to:

- become motivated to come together;
- understand the nature of its oppression;
- identify its requirements;
- plan its action; and
- take part in developing services and resources to the community.

Figure 3.2 provides a checklist of points which may be useful in
trying to oversome inertia and sustain interest.

As we will see below, a community profile can contribute signi-
ficantly to all of these processes, providing that the key principle
of allowing as much control and ownership of the process and
product by the community as possible is adhered to.

Figure 3.2 Overcoming inertia and sustaining interest

> - 'Apathy' is only a lack of interest; it is not necessarily a permanent state. Find out why there is little interest and how to stimulate motivation
> - Maintaining the enthusiasm of participants:
>   - make sure there is clarity of purpose
>   - don't spend forever talking about things
>   - get going quickly
>   - start small so that something can happen quite quickly
>   - avoid unnecessary bureaucracy or bureaucratic procedures
>   - wherever possible, make it fun!
> - Make sure that the community is kept involved at all stages of the project and that there is enough going on to sustain people's commitment and enthusiasm

Given such a potentially powerful tool in the community workers' kit bag, it is surprising to read, in a survey of local authority community work commissioned by the Department of Health and Social Security, that community workers do not commonly use community profiles. Although the study did find projects concerned with surveying local needs and services, it concluded that these were low in number. The report then went on to state that since there are no special resources required to conduct them apart from the workers' own skills, the activity is not regarded as an important one by the workers themselves.[3]

We would question the assumption that surveys do not require any special resources. Another possible explanation for the lack of profiling activity found by the researchers might be that they were looking for formal surveys resulting in standard reports to be used in the local authority planning process. The dominant community work approach at the time, however, was mistrustful of such overt intervention by agencies. A manual for community work supervisors had stated, five years earlier, that 'Survey methods can be the manipulation of a powerless and unsuspecting audience for ends that are opaque and with results that rarely get back to the providers of the data'.[4]

This suspicion was echoed more recently in an Association of Community Workers discussion paper on neighbourhood profiles:

Most people suspect that when a politician says 'we need more research on this subject' it is a strategy for delaying painful political action. When an academic says those words they can usually be translated, 'I would like to continue to earn a fat salary while doing some work which I find interesting and not too stressful or sweaty.' Why then should a Community Worker, a local community group, a voluntary organisation or a church ever want to do research on their locality or on an issue that affects it?[5]

However, those wishing to empower communities (and that can include politicians and academics) have used community profiles for a number of decades in a variety of ways which we explore in more depth in Chapter 9. They include using them as tools to facilitate community development and meet people, to assist campaigning and as a planning aid.

Community self-surveys

Community self-survey was an expression that became popular in the USA and the Netherlands in the 1950s. At that time, community development was seen principally in terms of motivating and educating communities so that they were able to make their own structural changes and self-surveys were seen as a means to these 'socio-pedagogic' ends. The authors of self-survey manuals assumed that although self-surveys might be sponsored by an agency, they were extensively controlled by the community, and this was seen as part of the learning process. 'The distinctive feature of the self-survey is that the citizens of a community are responsible for and participate in every phase of the investigation'.[6] Four years after Wormser wrote this in 1949, Sanders added: 'True advancement depends upon a knowledge of conditions: Learning starts with the familiar, the near at hand, the experienced; Facts have more interest and motivating power when you gather them yourself'.[7]

This concept of self-surveys, pioneered in the USA where whole cities were surveyed, never became popular on the same scale in Britain. In the 1970s, however, the technique was adopted by some such as Weiner, although here it was seen very much as a method for use by the community with no mention of a sponsoring agent. The reasons Weiner gives for a community conducting a self-survey are no longer pedagogic but rather:

(1) It can ask the questions that it wants to ask rather than those that the Government authorities or university department who normally runs surveys want answered. (2) The results of the survey remain the property of the community to be used as they think best. (3) As many as possible local people are involved in carrying it out.[8]

Empowerment is seen as coming through having control over the process, ownership of the profile and overcoming apathy.[9]

In the 1950s, self-surveys were conceived of as mirrors that a sponsoring agent helps the community to construct and hold up to itself.[10] In Britain that 'mirror' was often held up to the community not only so that it could change itself but to give it a sense of pride and history, to understand its own roots and as a means of celebration. Community arts projects which began to develop in the 1970s with these kind of aims now help communities to produce profiles as videos, exhibitions or books. One such group say in the introduction to their book: 'Yorkshire Art Circus believes that everyone has a story to tell, and this book was one way to encourage people in Upton, South Kirkby, Moorthorpe and South Elmsall to tell theirs . . . Communities cannot have too many books and if we have acted as a catalyst for discussion, and writing, that is praise indeed'.[11]

Degrees of community involvement

There are two issues relating to the appropriate level of community involvement that you ought to consider before embarking on a community profile. We have already touched on the issue of the level of participation and control by residents in relation to that of an outside agency; the other is the depth of involvement of individuals taking part. You will need to take a view on these issues in developing a strategy for involving the community in the practical work of the profile.

Balance of community and professional involvement

One way of conceptualizing the extent of community involvement as opposed to professional involvement is to see the community-profiling project as either a top-down exercise, where the profile is essentially carried out by outsiders with perhaps some consultation with community leaders, or as a bottom-up exercise, where the community itself takes charge of the profiling process. In practice, there are a range of possibilities between these two extremes that combine both the skill and expertise of the professional with the local knowledge and enthusiasm of residents, both of which are likely to be important ingredients of a successful community profile.

If the profile is to be taken seriously, especially by those in positions of authority who are responsible for allocating resources, then it needs to be seen to be undertaken as systematically and professionally as resources will allow. However, this should not be an overriding consideration that stifles participants' creativity and spontaneity. As we are at pains to point out, community involvement is important to the process and it can also help to furnish the finished product with colour and an insight that outsiders may find more difficult to supply. Therefore, there ideally needs to be a balance between the more objective, expert assistance from outside agencies and the enthusiastic, insider understanding of the community itself.

Deciding on the appropriate balance

There is no rule about the extent to which the community should be involved in the process of undertaking a community profile. As with all aspects of undertaking the profile, it is important to consider the following: What is the community profile for? What constitutes the community to be profiled? What methods are to be used? What resources are available? These will now be discussed in turn.

Perhaps the first set of questions to ask is: Why are you undertaking the profile at all? What do you (and others) want from it? Is the proposed level of involvement by the community and others in accordance with your aims and objectives? This is especially important if one of the aims of the project is to empower the community.

We have already seen that the concept of the community is complex. Among the questions you need to ask in formulating a strategy for community involvement are: What or who constitutes the community? Who are the key actors who are already most involved in the community? Who could help deliver the profile? Are there divisions within the community that should be taken account of? It may well be that a particular group of residents would refuse to participate if a certain agency or professional was to be involved. The converse might also happen as when a vicar we were working with on a project refused to allow 'his' parish hall to be used for a meeting by one part of the community.

Chapters 4–6 explore a range of methods which are available for undertaking community profiles. Your choice of the most appropriate method will depend largely on the aims of the profile and the resources available; however, those decisions are also related to the degree of community involvement required. For example, it may be the case that you want the profile to take the form of a video that celebrates the development and current activities of a community. There is no doubt that such a project would depend for its success on the participation of local people in writing the script, stage directing, 'acting' themselves, making editorial decisions and so on. However, unless you have considerable skills in camera work, lighting and sound recording, dubbing and mixing, within the community the video may not be watchable. This suggests that some 'professional' or 'expert' assistance is required in addition to the participation of members of the community.

Underpinning many of these decisions will be the availability of resources in order to undertake the profile to the standard you require. We have considered the availability of key people among residents, people who work within the community and also other experts who you can call upon, and the skills that they have at their disposal. You also need to consider the availability of money to employ people who require payment, and also the time within which the profile is to be completed. You may need to weigh in the balance the desire to undertake a professional, systematic profile in a short space of time against the wish to involve local people, provide training in necessary skills and retain a greater level of control over the process.

Three tiers of community involvement

A further dimension to consider when planning the level of community involvement, is what is entailed in individuals' participation. There are perhaps three levels at which individuals can get involved, although in practice the categories are blurred (see Fig. 3.3). The first level is that of the wider community where you can involve everyone even if it is only to tell them about the profile

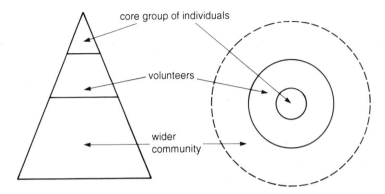

Figure 3.3   Three tiers of community involvement

and ask if they wish to contribute. The second level is that of those
members of the community who may volunteer to help in a more
practical way in assisting the process. You may wish also to
develop a core group of individuals who will plan and manage the
profiling process.

Wider community
You can involve the wider community in your community profile
in two ways: first, by keeping everyone informed about each stage
of the process and, secondly, through gathering information from
as many members of the community as possible. Keeping the
community informed about how the profile is progressing is important for a number of reasons. In the initial stages, there may be
considerable suspicion of the motives of those organizing the
profile: Who are they? Where are they from? Why are they
interested in us? It is important therefore to explain clearly what
the profile is for, how it will be undertaken and the timetable of
events. Later in the process it may be necessary to inform the
community about the preliminary findings, perhaps to check that
no major mistakes or misinterpretations have been made. Finally,
when the report has been completed you can give the results back
to the community in a form that is accessible and understandable
(see Chapter 9).

Many people undertaking profiles prepare a press release or a
leaflet before, during and possibly after the process, and this
basic publicity can be supplemented with conveniently placed, eye-
catching posters and by ensuring that as many people as possible

are talking – in an informed way – about the profile. Pubs, post offices, bingo nights at the community centre and outside the school are all good places to start passing the word out about what is happening. You can also inform the community about the findings through newsletters, exhibitions and displays (see Chapter 9).

Another way you can involve the wider community is by obtaining information and opinion directly from members of the community. Methods for obtaining primary data are explored in Chapters 5 and 6, although particular attention should be drawn to those methods that seek to involve as many residents as possible, such as surveys. There are several techniques you can use for maximizing participation in surveys, such as running a free prize draw to encourage completion of questionnaires, inviting responses to initial findings through the inclusion of tear-off slips attached to newsletters or leaflets, and the organization of discussion groups around particular themes and issues.[12] Figure 3.4 provides some hints on contacting groups in the community.

Volunteers
The next level at which people might be involved is that of practical assistance in the work of undertaking the profile. There is usually a pool of people within any community who would like to do something different or to make better use of their skills. Many just see it as a good opportunity to meet their neighbours and get to know more about their community. Offering people a practical task may be an effective way of involving them. Many people do not like groups that 'only sit around and talk'; they are the active

Figure 3.4   Working with existing groups or forming new groups

- It is often difficult to get people to come to public meetings. So, to begin with, work through established groups such as parent and toddler groups, elderly persons' lunch clubs, centres for the unemployed, youth groups, etc.
- Use established channels of communications and networks
- Watch out for the pitfalls of utilizing existing groups, e.g. avoid cliques and involve everyone
- If there is little community organization currently in existence, then write into the planning process time and resources for community development

people who want to get going, and there is always plenty to be done. The knowledge and skills needed can range from quite high-level computer technology to making the tea and can include mapping, interviewing, word processing, drawing cartoons, designing lay-outs for reports and posters, chairing public meetings, leafleting and talking to the press.

Many of these skills can be learned quickly and becoming involved in community profiling offers a good opportunity for people to acquire them if a suitable instructor can be found. However, there may be people, perhaps retired, who already have such skills and knowledge. It is therefore valuable to have a pool of volunteers with a wide range of skills available that can be called on within the community.

There are three further issues that you will need to consider in developing a strategy for community involvement. The first is confidentiality. Members of the community may be unhappy about providing personal information to people they know, for example during interviews as part of a survey. This will need to be considered in making decisions about using members of the community to undertake interview work. The second issue is whether to pay volunteers for their work on the profile. If you have funds available, paying key people a part-time wage can be seen as a way of ensuring a consistent level of input, although there may be a danger of others who are not paid refusing to become involved.

The third issue relates to the balance between, on the one hand, training and supervising people in the community to undertake certain tasks and, on the other, paying a 'professional' to do the work for you. While the first method will help to increase such skills within the community and will ensure a higher degree of community involvement in the process, it will also take longer and is likely to require considerable person power.[13]

Core group of individuals
The community as a whole cannot undertake a profile; a meeting of a few hundred people would find it hard to make decisions. Also, not everyone who wants to be involved is happy in meetings or wishes to have a say in organizing the process. There is, however, a need for someone, or preferably a small group, to make the decisions and plan and organize the process, and make sure things happen on time. In profiles covering single issues or small areas, the project steering 'group' may be just one individual, but

generally there will be a group of people involved (see Chapter 2). For all the reasons outlined earlier (giving a sense of ownership and control, intimate knowledge of the issues, having positive practical support and so on), it is preferable that that group or committee involves, if it is not composed entirely of, people from the community.

How are these people selected? In most cases, they will be self-selected; perhaps they are the originators of the profile or have responded to invitations to join the committee. However, when you are putting together a committee, some attention should be paid to ensuring that all sections of the community are represented, and that as far as possible those people do represent others. For example, members from existing groups such as ethnic minority associations or area youth committees may wish to take part, or steering group members could be elected from different parts of an estate. A steering group, especially when it becomes the management group (see Chapter 2), is the driving force behind the profile, and should provide others with motivation and enthusiasm. The involvement of the community in the group can go a long way towards helping that process.

Some larger community profiles may employ a project worker to take them forward. Especially when a profile is initiated by a statutory body such as a local authority department, this role may be filled by someone from that agency. However this post is filled, it is important that the project worker's role is seen as a coordinating one that facilitates rather than frustrates community involvement. It is especially important that the project worker has clear lines of accountability.

Involving the community throughout all stages

Having considered the possible levels of community involvement, we can now turn to the stages of the community-profiling process at which the community might be involved. We refer the reader to the stages identified in Fig. 2.1, which we will now consider in turn.

Preparing the ground

Once the process of undertaking a community profile has become more than an idea, you will need to take steps to prepare the ground. As in all preparatory work, this stage will set the foundation on which the rest of the process rests, so it is important to get it right. In order to do so you need to involve the community both to ensure its support and also provide essential information.

A steering group needs to be set up as early as possible along the lines described in Chapter 2, involving at least some members of the community, and ensuring that *all* sections of the community are in some way represented, if at all possible. In putting together members of the steering group, you need to consider the following issues: Will the community support the steering group? How will it be seen by the community? Are the members well respected?

The initial planning of the profile should involve the community in considerations about what are the boundaries of the community to be profiled and what defines the community. Initial contacts should be made with as many local groups and key individuals as possible, such as community activists, social organizers and locally based professionals. Are they supportive of the idea to undertake a profile? What can they offer? Have they any further suggestions about the process that have not yet been considered? In identifying the resources that exist within the community that can be mobilized on behalf of the profile, it is important to include members of the community who have relevant skills: market research, photography, computing, design and lay-out skills, and so on. Do any groups, organizations or individuals have a computer that can be used? Are there meeting places for both small and large meetings? Initial clarification of the aims and objectives need to be checked out with the community. What exactly is the purpose of the profile? Who owns it? Who is controlling it?

Once a steering group has been established, and some of the key people contacted, it is time to ensure that the wider community is approached. Publicity can take a variety of forms, the most usual being leaflets, posters and press releases (see Fig. 3.5). Whatever form of publicity you choose, you should ensure that you address the following issues: Does your information tell people exactly what is happening, why, when, how, and who is doing it? Is it short, to the point and readable? Does it need to be in languages other than English? Can leaflets be put through everyone's door, and how else can they be distributed?[14]

Figure 3.5 Publicity

> - Make use of the local press, TV and radio to publicize the project and also to keep people informed of progress throughout
> - Let people know what is happening, and sound out ideas, by going to where people meet – outside schools, pubs, post offices on pension days, and so on

Fieldwork and reporting

After the preparation comes the main part of the process, that is, the fieldwork. This involves gathering all the information, from primary or secondary sources, putting it together and analysing it, then producing a draft profile. Much of the emphasis on involvement by the community in the preparatory stage was through the steering group. In this stage, volunteers can make a significant input to the work, although the steering group or management group will still be making some decisions and the wider community will be involved through supplying much of the information.[15]

You can involve volunteers in all aspects of data collection, collation and analysis. Those who already have relevant skills will of course be invaluable, but the profile can offer a rare opportunity for other willing residents to acquire new skills and experience. What skills are required for your particular profile? Can they be taught? Are there people or organizations willing to pass on those skills?

If you intend to use local volunteers, there are a number of issues that you need to consider. What is the best method of recruiting them? You can do this through word-of-mouth, personal contacts, posters or advertising in the local paper or job centre. Are you going to interview applicants or will you welcome any volunteer? Should you pay them? If so, it could be per day or for discrete pieces of work such as a certain amount for each interview. Some profiles have offered volunteers a 'reward' for their help, others have even offered such 'rewards' to all interviewees. What level of training will the volunteers need, and who will provide it? How will the fieldwork be coordinated and who, if necessary, will supervise it? We look at some issues relating to the recruitment and training of interviewers in more detail in Chapter 6.

Community involvement is crucial when you are drafting and

piloting the questionnaire. It will ensure that the questionnaire addresses issues that have salience for members of the community to be profiled and in a way that has meaning for them. Is the language used and the way places and things are referred to locally relevant? Are the issues ones that residents will respond to, and enjoy answering?

Your draft profile can of course be altered later, but this may be the first output of the process and will give an important impression of it. It is important, therefore, that you ensure that as far as possible it is clear and acceptable to the community and others who it is aimed at. Community representatives may have a particular role to play in interpreting data, so it is worth seeking their views on the possible reasons for especially surprising findings. Are there any verbatim comments that can enliven the report? Ideally, a draft report needs to be discussed by the community that is its focus. This can be achieved through a series of public meetings or by presenting key findings at a public exhibition and inviting comments or by delivering a summary sheet with a slip for comments or simply through the feedback from the community representatives involved in the project. When you have made any further changes the final profile can be produced. As with the draft report, it is very important to ensure that everyone who contributed has a copy, or access to a copy, and that members of the wider community are aware that the profile has been produced.

Action

Once you have completed all the fieldwork and have produced the community profile, it is time to do something with it. What that is will largely depend on the original aims and objectives, but also on any changes that have been made to those in the course of the process, possibly as a result of the input by the community. Whatever uses the profile will be put to, it is likely to affect the community in some way, perhaps through campaigning for additional resources or changes in service provision, or merely to enlighten and raise the awareness of members of the community and decision makers about issues relevant to that community. As members of the community are likely to be affected by the profile, it is essential that they have a further opportunity to become involved at this stage.

It is of course important that you involve the community in whatever event you use to launch the profile and in developments that occur as a result. You should also find some means to feed back to the community the findings of the profile. We explore some of these uses and the potential for community involvement further in Chapter 9.

Key issues

In this chapter, we have explored some of the issues that face those intending to undertake a profile when considering how best to encourage active involvement by the community. Initially, you need to have a clear understanding of the overall structure of the community that is the subject of the profile: What are the divisions, conflicts and power structures? What are the common bonds? Where are the boundaries? What are the bases for the social and cultural networks? With that understanding you can develop the aims and objectives of the profile and check them with the community.

You then need to understand and be aware of the methods and processes of undertaking the exercise, and especially of the potential effects that professional assistance can have on the community. Like many services offered to a community, a community profile can serve to further repress and control the community, or it can become a powerful tool in assisting the process of education and liberation. All sections of the defined community should be heard; but it is not only important for you to listen to what members of the community are saying, but also to involve them in a meaningful way in the process itself.

Finally therefore, issues of ownership and management of the whole process are important. If members of the community are in any way to control it, what mechanisms should there be? It is essential that you involve the widest section of the community as possible, and from these members draw on the resources of both a group of voluntary helpers, and individuals who can form, or become part of, the steering group. In turn, those volunteers or core group members must find ways of being accountable to that wider community. There must be adequate and sensitive support and training for those who need it and also sufficient time allocated for the profile to proceed at a pace that will maintain the maximum amount of community involvement.

Further reading

Beresford, P. and Croft, S. (1993) *Citizen Involvement: A Practical Guide for Change*. London: British Association of Social Workers/ Macmillan.

Burns, D. (1991) 'Ladder of participation', *Going Local*, No. 18, Summer.

Institute of Housing/TPAS (1989) *Tenant Participation in Housing Management*. Coventry: IOH/TPAS.

Rees, S. (1991) *Achieving Power: Practice and Policy in Social Welfare*, London: Allen and Unwin.

Smith, M. (1981) *Organise*, Leicester: National Association of Youth Clubs.

Notes

1. For example, Bromsgrove and Redditch District Health Authority commissioned a profile into *People Living in Bromsgrove and Redditch Health Authority Aged 16–64 Years with Severe Physical Disability* (Hereford and Worcester County Council 1989).
2. Haggstrom, W.C. (1970) 'The psychological implications of the community development process'. In *Community Development as a Process* (L.J. Cary, ed.). Columbia, MO: University of Missouri Press.
3. Department of Health and Social Security (1982) *Local Authority Community Work: Realities of Practice*. London: HMSO.
4. Briscoe, C. and Henderson, D.N. (1977) *Community Work: Learning and Supervision*. National Institute of Social Services Library No. 32. London: George Allen and Unwin.
5. Smith, G. (1983) *Neighbourhood Profiles: Surveys and the Census*. Association of Community Workers Talking Points No. 142. Newcastle: Association of Community Workers.
6. Wormser, M.H. (1949) 'The Northtown Self-survey: A case study, *Journal of Social Issues*, Vol. 5, No. 2.
7. Sanders, I.T. (1953) *Making Good Communities Better*. Lexington, KY: University of Kentucky Press.
8. Weiner, R. (1972) *Community Self-survey: A Do It Yourself Guide*. Belfast: Northern Ireland Community Relations Commission.
9. Village appraisal as advocated by parish councils and rural community councils is a more recent form of self-survey that has been facilitated by the development of the software package *Village Appraisal*, described in Chapters 4 and 7.
10. Lippitt, R., Watson, J. and Westley, B. (1958) *The Dynamics of Planned Change: A Comparative Study of Principles and Techniques*. New York: Harcourt, Brace and World.

11. Griffiths, L. *et al.* (1988) *Communities Under the Hammer: Privy to Privatisation*. Castleford: Yorkshire Arts Council.
12. The *Bloomsbury Safety Audit* (Safe Estates for Women (1992) was produced by local women who, with the help of a development worker, conducted a 'planning for real' exercise, made a video highlighting the problems of the estate, had a walkabout with officials and undertook a priority search survey defined and administered by residents. See Chapter 5 for using a variety of data-gathering techniques.
13. Profiles that used local volunteers include the *Bloomsbury Safety Audit* (Safe Estates for Women 1992), the *Walton Parish Council Local Study 1984* (Walton Parish Council 1984) and the *Howden Community Needs Survey* (Communicate 1990).
14. Communicate's (1990) *Howden Community Needs Study* (Newcastle Upon Type: Communicate) went through the process of designing the study with the local community forum.
15. The *Abbeyview Consultation Paper* (Fife Region and Dunfermline District Councils 1992), *Taking Books to People* (Backhouse and Burton 1986) and the *City Challenge Health Project* (City Challenge Health Project 1992), all provide examples of involving residents at the fieldwork stage.

4

Making use of existing information

Introduction

> Information can be compared to a bad road full of holes and bumps so that it is impossible to drive on it. The holes and bumps represent the missing and incorrect or misleading information . . . however even a bad road is passable (usable) to the careful driver.[1]

Before undertaking any primary research, one of the first activities of a community profile should be to gather together existing data and information about the area under study – so-called secondary research. Whatever the community being profiled, there is almost certainly some information somewhere that could be helpful. A careful search for, and use of, this information will save time and money that would otherwise be spent collecting primary data. Indeed, in our 'information society' there is sometimes information overload and so it is important that the information you collect is relevant to the aims and objectives of the profile and that you engage in a systematic search for such relevant material.

There are a number of benefits in using secondary information.[2] Secondary data are cheap, often readily accessible, and analysis can be undertaken relatively quickly. Using secondary data can often allow you to examine past trends and make comparisons with other groups or places that would not be possible for a single researcher undertaking primary research. Indeed, some profiles are based entirely on secondary quantitative data. These are often produced by local authorities or health authorities and include most of the secondary statistics that are available on an area basis such as wards or postcodes. This is, of course, far cheaper than surveying the populations of their district which, in any case, may not be feasible in terms of time and resources. The main problems involved in gathering existing information are finding out precisely what information is available, identifying where it is located and then getting access to it. Your local library is a good starting point in collecting the information you need. Librarians should also be able to help you develop a search strategy for collecting existing information.

There are two basic approaches to collecting secondary data. One can either think of all potential data sources and then approach them to collect any data that are relevant to the community under study, or one could take a more focused approach: identify the aims of the profile and then look for the information required to support these aims. One needs to decide what data are required and how they can be obtained. It is also sensible to think about what comparative data may be needed to make sense of the community profile.

This chapter examines both quantitative and qualitative information; it looks at their uses and sources before concluding with a brief discussion on how to interpret such information.

Types of information

Information or data can be described as being 'hard' or 'soft', or 'quantitative' or 'qualitative'. 'Hard' data can be described as 'quality information', that is, information about which we are confident.[3] It is usually quantified, that is, it takes the form of statistics. Soft, or qualitative, data on the other hand, do not allow statistical precision but often explore subjective aspects of people's experiences; the feelings and attitudes that lie behind statistics.

Quantitative information

Quantitative information is useful in a community profile for a variety of reasons (see Fig. 4.1). It can be used to *identify the population to be surveyed*. If you are unsure where or who you want to include in your profile, you may want to use available statistics to look at which area(s) of group(s) within a community are the most appropriate for you to study. This will be particularly important for local authorities and health authorities, who will often not be able to profile the whole of their administrative area and will have to choose which community or communities they wish to profile in detail. Using available statistics, it is possible to

Figure 4.1   Uses of existing statistics

- Identify population to be surveyed
- Check representativeness of survey sample
- Complement primary information
- Compare community with other areas
- Create a context for the research

identify, for example, those groups or communities experiencing the most ill health or the highest unemployment.

If you undertake a sample survey you will want *to check how representative your sample is* of the wider community (see section on sampling in Chapter 6). You will therefore need secondary data to provide some approximation of the composition of the local community, for example with regard to gender or ethnic composition and age structure, against which to check your own sample characteristics.

Existing statistics can be used when writing up your report to *complement the primary information you have collected*. You can use this existing information to support arguments, to make points and to help illustrate community needs. For example, if your survey finds that a significant number of respondents suffer from poor health, then you can use secondary information from the health authority to corroborate this. In one community profile undertaken by the authors, it was found that the community had high levels of self-reported illness. Secondary data showed that the area had a high standardized mortality ratio, the highest number of reported cases of many infectious diseases in the district, and an increasing number of low-birthweight babies. This information added weight to the argument that action was needed on health.[4]

Another use of existing data is *to make comparisons and create a context* for your community profile. 'Properly used, numbers provide by far the most effective way of describing change or making comparisons'.[5] Quantitative information can be used to make comparisons with other localities, regions, or the country as a whole. In order to do this, of course, the information you have has to be available for these other places in a comparable form. The census of population is one of the best sources of information for this type of use as it covers the whole of the UK. In addition, many sources of secondary statistics, such as the number of people unemployed, are available at different geographical levels, often right down to postcode level. It is possible, then, to say how a community compares with the rest of the locality, the region, the country or, indeed, how different groups within the community compare with each other. While sources such as *Social Trends*[6] are not disaggregated to the local level, they can still be used for context and to compare the community with the country as a whole. Moreover, *Regional Trends*[7] provides extensive data which can be used to see how the community compares with the region.

Sources of quantitative information

This section aims to identify information that you might find useful and gives some guidance on where you might be able to obtain it. When approaching organizations for information, it is sensible to ask for the research, information or statistics section of the relevant organization and to be as clear as possible about what information you require and why. All local authority departments, local health agencies and other public sector agencies will be listed in alphabetical order in the local telephone directory and in the community section at the front of the *Thomsons Directory*. Voluntary organizations should be traceable through the local Council for Voluntary Services.

Your first task should be to find out whether any research has been undertaken on your community in the past. Was it on the community as a whole or part of a larger survey? Who undertook the research? Do you have access to the results? This may provide answers to some of your questions or suggest issues that you need to examine in your profile. It is important to contact your local authority, health authority, training and enterprise council, university or college to see if anyone has undertaken any research that is relevant to your project.

In the rest of this section we provide, for each type of information, guidance as to what you can obtain and from which source(s).

Characteristics of the population
Information about the composition of your community is important irrespective of the precise purpose of your community profile. How many people are in the community? How old are they? What sex are they? What ethnic groups do they belong to? How many

have a disability? What is the structure of households in the community?

Your main source of information here will be the census of population. This takes place every ten years and, in principle, asks everyone in the UK a number of questions about themselves, their household, their employment and other characteristics. All residents are required by law to complete the census questionnaire and failure to complete a questionnaire, or deliberately to complete it wrongly, can lead to a fine. As a consequence, it is the most comprehensive source of basic population information. The results are used by government departments and public sector organizations, such as local authorities and health authorities, in planning services and allocating resources. The census of population asks everyone their age, sex, marital status, who they live with, where they were living one year ago, where they were born, what ethnic group they consider they belong to, and whether they have a long-term illness or disability that limits their daily activities.

The census of population has the advantage for those involved in profiling geographically defined communities that it can generate results for very small geographical areas, called enumeration districts, usually consisting of about 200 households. The census is also available on local authority ward, district and county level and by postcode. In consequence, your community can be readily compared to other communities and the country as a whole to determine its relative position.

The results of the census of population are available from a number of sources. Her Majesty's Stationery Office (HMSO)[8] produce guides for every county which include the main results broken down by local authority district. Information on a local authority area and particular wards within it should be available from its planning department. The local health authority should also have full census results for the district it covers. OPCS Customer Services[9] are also able to assist.

The census of population only occurs once every ten years and the results take time to be analysed and disseminated. The full results of the 1991 census were not available until 1993. So, if you were undertaking a community profile in 1992, the chances are you were using census data that was 11 years old. Given the extent of changes that typically occur over a decade, it is highly likely that these figures no longer give an accurate picture of the community. So, if you are undertaking a community profile more than, say, five years after the last census, it is worth checking with your local authority planning department to see whether they have any more up-to-date figures. They may, for example, have undertaken their own mid-census population survey or they may have made use of the OPCS mid-year population estimates.

Local economy/labour market

Information about employment, skills and training in your community may be an important part of the profile. You may want to know about the 'supply' side of the labour market – how many people are in work and what they do; how many people are out of work and for how long; how many people are in further or higher education; how many people are on training schemes and so on. Looking at the 'demand' side, you may want to know who the local employers are, what they do, how the local economy has changed in recent years, how many vacancies there are, how many redundancies there have been and so on.

For information on the local economy and local labour market, the key source of information will be your local Training and Enterprise Council (TEC), which produces an annual 'Labour Market Assessment' which analyses the condition of the local labour market and covers issues such as employment, unemployment, training, education and small firms. The TEC will also have commissioned additional research on the local labour market and will have data relating to how well the area is performing in relation to the National Training Targets. The TEC also has access to labour market information through the National Online Manpower Information System (NOMIS), which is the main source of official labour market information in the UK. It provides unemployment, vacancy, population and census of employment (see below) data at local authority district level and, for some statistics, at lower levels such as wards and postcodes. Accessing this information requires knowledge of the system and some computing skills and it could be costly. It is possible that researchers in social science departments or research units at your local university, however, will have access to it. NOMIS will undertake analysis of this information for you if you cannot obtain it from other sources.[10] The census of employment is a survey of employers that takes place every three years. It can provide information on the numbers of local workplaces by broad industry group and number of employees in these industries. The results are usually available at local authority district and county level.

Your local authority economic development unit will also have access to local economy and labour market information and is also likely to monitor openings/closures of companies. Much of this information may be provided in its economic strategy or annual plan. The local authority planning department will also have useful information which it uses in the preparation of its Unitary Development Plan.

The census of population also asks questions of relevance to the local economy. People have to give details about their labour market status, whether they had undertaken any paid work in the past week, whether they had undertaken any paid work in the past 10 years, present or previous job title and main tasks, business of employer, location of workplace, how they travel to work, and any degrees, professional qualifications or vocational qualifications held. The regional office of the Employment Service has an employment intelligence unit which may also have relevant information and may produce regional labour market analyses. Other possible sources include your local low pay unit (if there is one) and the local chamber of commerce. They may be able to provide you with information about firms in the local economy and how the local economy is performing. They often undertake business surveys and may then have useful statistics on future prospects and business confidence. There may be an inner-city task force, development corporation or local development agency in your area which may also be able to provide information about issues relating to the local economy.

Housing

Housing is an important aspect of people's lives and is likely, therefore, to be included in a community profile. Where do people live? Who owns the property? How much does it cost to live there? Can people afford to buy their own homes? How easy is it to get a house or flat? These are all questions which you may want to consider. You may need information on tenure (owner-occupied or rented from a private landlord, local authority or housing association), the types of homes people live in (flats, terraces, semi-detached maisonettes, detached, etc.), housing costs (local house prices, rent levels, rent arrears, numbers of people in receipt of housing benefit), evidence of housing need (homelessness, local authority waiting lists, levels of overcrowding) and the housing stock, including the state of repair of housing and vacant properties.

The census of population contains some information about housing including type, number of rooms, who owns the property, whether the home has central heating and whether it is used, whether it has an internal toilet and whether it has a bath or shower.

The local authority housing department will also have information on the properties it owns, as should any local housing associations. The housing department will also have information on homelessness, housing benefit, waiting lists, stock condition, area renewal status, rent arrears and may also have carried out a tenant satisfaction study. The local authority finance department should have information on council tax levels in the area and this will provide some information on the relative market value of properties. Local estate agents may have information on local house prices and will often have a good overview of the local housing market. Citizens' advice bureaux collect information on numbers of people seeking advice on housing issues and the campaigning group, Shelter, often have local offices where you will be able to get information on housing issues in the area.

Education
How do children fare in local schools? What prospects do they have? The newly published school league tables provide information on the success of pupils in examinations. However, these have come in for considerable criticism on the following grounds. They are incomplete because three out of four private schools boycotted their compilation and sixth-form and further education colleges are not included. Some of the results were wrongly recorded as confirmed by the erratum slips that were sent out with them. The results are misleading as they do not take into account the background or the different educational starting points of pupils. They ignore other important aspects of education such as the personal development or social skills of pupils.[11] However, they are available and can be used (carefully) in a profile if required. They are likely to be improved in the near future with the addition of data on 'value added', correcting for some of the above problems.

Information about issues such as the number of children receiving free school meals, entitlement to school uniform allowance, education maintenance allowance and school transport should be available from the local education authority. This information may indicate levels of financial hardship among families locally and, taken together with the school league table and other relevant information, give an initial picture of the local school and those who attend it. You may also want to obtain other information such as pupil:teacher ratios and the number of places at local schools. Information about further education provision should be available from your local TEC.

The local careers service should also be able to provide information about the destination of school leavers and may have additional information on issues like career aspirations, youth training and unemployment rates among school leavers.

Health
What is the main cause of death? Is it preventable? How healthy are babies, how many die in the first year of life, how many are born underweight? These are all important indicators of the state of health of a community. The standardized mortality ratio (SMR) is a standardized index that allows one to compare causes of death in different localities. It will be available from your local health authority and can be used to make comparisons between communities and with districts, regions or the country as a whole.

Another useful indicator is the infant mortality rate, which can also be obtained from the health authority. This gives some indication not only of the health of mothers and babies, but it is also used as an indicator of social progress, in that it reflects the experiences of the most vulnerable member of society who are likely to the first affected by any deterioration in their living conditions.

You may also want information on health services available to the community including GPs, dentists, clinics, community nurses, hospitals and so on. The regional health authority, NHS Trust and family health services will all have information on services for which they are responsible and the community health council will also be able to help you and may be more approachable. Local health centres or GPs may also have also relevant information. The census of population provides information on those who are long-term sick and those who are permanently disabled.

Environment
There may be a range of environmental issues that you want to address in your community profile including: What are the levels of pollution? What is local land used for? How safe are the roads? What is the quality of the local environment? How much refuse is

collected and how much is recycled? What is the quality of air or water?

Your local authority environmental health department should have some information on these issues and a local Friends of the Earth branch may also have undertaken relevant research or environmental monitoring. The highways department of the local authority will have details on traffic accidents and the water authority information on water quality. Information on land use should be available from the local authority planning department and future plans for the use of that land will be contained in the authority's Unitary Development Plan. Another issue relating to the safety of the environment is crime. The police authority for your area will produce statistics on different kinds of crime for each sub division on beat area.

Community services
In considering the resources available within a community, you will need to take account of the range and quality of services provided to that community. These might include shops, banks, public transport, social and welfare services, leisure and community facilities. While much of this information you will have to collect yourselves, local authority departments should be able to supply information on the services they provide; most produce annual reports which are a starting point. Other relevant sources include the local passenger transport authority and local traders' associations. You may be able to get some information on the quality of local services from satisfaction surveys, which increasing numbers of local authority departments are now conducting.

Poverty and welfare
Many of the sources already mentioned will indicate levels of poverty and disadvantage in the community. Unemployment will provide some information, as will numbers of people on housing benefits and the proportions of pupils getting free school meals. Other indicators might include the numbers of house repossessions, the levels of rent arrears and the numbers of disconnections of gas and electricity. Information on the numbers of people on income support may be available from your local social security office. Unfortunately, data on personal income is not available from the Inland Revenue.

Information about the types of problems facing people may be available from local citizens' advice bureaux (CABs), which should have information on caseloads – the numbers of people contacting their local CAB on a particular subject. Information on disconnections will be available from bodies such as the Office for Electricity Regulation (OFFER) and the Office of Water Services (OFFWAT). The utility providers themselves will also have this information. Social services departments will have details of children in care, and details of clients and the services they receive. They may also have undertaken a survey of clients' needs.

Qualitative information

Qualitative information can provide an additional dimension to the profile. While subjective it provides insights into attitudes, beliefs, feelings, impressions and opinions. Using qualitative information can often bring a community profile to life and the use of graphic images also helps. Some people 'turn off' at the presentation of statistics on their own, while others are wary of them as they can be manipulated, massaged and misused.

Qualitative information has at least three key uses. First, it can help *identify local issues* and may help decide what issues you need to cover in your primary research. Second, it can provide *new insights and ideas* and throw new light on quantitative information. Third, it can *bring clarity and vivid illustration to the profile*: a letter to a local paper, a photograph of poor housing can often convey more than statistics. If, say, 60 per cent of housing is substandard, then a photograph of crumbling walls and a quote from parents about the effect of their damp house on the health of their child can add emphasis to the point and help readers understand the realities behind the statistics.

Sources of qualitative information

It is often more difficult to trace qualitative information than it is to trace quantitative data, as its sources are usually much more varied. The sources indicated in Fig. 4.2 are not exhaustive, but they do cover the main ones that you may wish to use.

Newspapers
Local newspapers and magazines may be a good source of information on local issues. If the publisher has a library, it may be able to provide you with information on your community from its own index of cuttings. Alternatively, a local history library may

Figure 4.2   Sources of qualitative information

- Local newspapers and magazines
- Minutes/agendas of meetings
- Diaries/memos/meeting notes of local workers
- Projects in educational establishments
- Photographs
- Videos

have back copies which may be indexed so that you can trace relevant articles. Your local university or library may also keep back copies of papers and store national newspapers on compact discs, which can be searched for local stories.

Meetings of agencies
Minutes and agendas of meetings together with background reports for local organizations such as the local authority (and its various committees) and health authority should be available. These often deal with issues of prime concern to local communities. The public library should have minutes of all local authority committee meetings and many local authorities allow public access to relevant papers.

Diaries/memos/meeting notes of local workers
In one community profile undertaken by the authors, we were fortunate enough to have access to the meeting notes and memos sent and received by a key local worker. This information would not have been available from other sources and provided insight into 'behind-the-scenes' events from which most of us are normally excluded. This type of information can say something about the quality and delivery of local services and local needs and issues facing the community, as perceived by local workers.

Projects in educational institutions
These include projects undertaken by local school pupils, students on professional courses, local college or university students, student nurses, librarians, social workers or any other person who undertakes a project on the community as part of their education. Student nurses, for example, often have to undertake health profiles of particular communities and this information may be a useful addition to the community profile. University students often have to undertake projects for undergraduate or postgraduate

courses which may involve work in a particular community. School children may undertake a class project on 'Where I live'.

Photographs
Photographs can often illustrate what words cannot ('I can't describe how dirty the environment is'). Pictures can also show positive aspects of community life such as successful community events. You may wish to approach a local newspaper or ask local people for relevant photographs.

Videos
With the advent of the camcorder, home-produced videos are increasingly accessible. Does anyone within the community have a video? Is there any footage from the local news studio that can be used? Has a documentary ever been produced on your community?

Interpreting secondary statistics

There is a bewildering variety of official and unofficial data sources available to the local and regional research worker. However, most are limited by their spatial coverage, level of spatial disaggregation, frequency and completeness.[12]

Once the available, relevant statistics have been tracked down, they now have to interpreted: 'facts do not speak for themselves [they] have to be interpreted and analyzed'.[13] Some of the questions you might want to ask when confronted with a set of statistics are summarized in Fig. 4.3. Other factors one should take into account are discussed below.

Figure 4.3   Questions to ask when faced with a statistic[14]

- Who says so? Or who has undertaken and who has written about the research?
- How do they know? Or what method has been used and what is the sample?
- What's missing? Or what information is not there? What statistics are not given?
- Did somebody change the subject? Or does the result answer what the question asks?
- Does it make sense? Or has the assumption the statistic is based on been proved?

Are the data valid? Do the data measure what they are supposed to measure. For example, official 'unemployment' figures actually refer to the numbers of people claiming benefit. Unemployed people not eligible for benefit are excluded and some unemployed people not searching for work may be included. There can also be a problem in distinguishing between inputs, outputs and outcomes. In the health field, for example, the provision of health care could be measured by the ratio of health workers to population. This is an input. However, it may be better to look at an output measure of health care, such as levels of treatment or procedures carried out. Measures of access, too, are generally better than measures of the level of provision. For example, hospital waiting lists are more useful than the number of consultants. In practice, it is often only possible to have information relating to inputs and information about outcomes is rarely widely available without primary research and, continuing the health example, such outcome data might relate to the health of patients following treatment.

Are the data reliable? Will the procedure used to collect the information give similar results over time and in different situations? One should be wary of information that is collected predominately for administrative purposes. The unemployment figures are, again, a good example. Someone who was regarded as 'officially' unemployed in 1980 may not be officially unemployed, and therefore not included in statistics, in 1993.

Is the information complete? For example, information on crime is unlikely to be complete as various studies, such as the British Crime Survey, have discovered that many crimes go unreported and that the crime figures are likely to under-report the true level of crime.

What geographical area do the data cover? An important problem faced when undertaking a community profile is that there is usually a discrepancy between the area(s) for which information is available and the area covered by the profile. For example, when dealing with a particular geographic community such as a housing estate, while information will be available from a variety of sources, none will probably be an exact 'fit' with the area. Communities, especially where they are self-defined, do not normally fit ward boundaries, postcode areas, police subdivisions, health districts or local authority service boundaries. Moreover, information produced by various local agencies is often compiled at different levels: some may use wards, others postcodes, others their own boundaries. One can end up collecting a great deal of information that does not fit very well. Hence the importance of undertaking primary research.

The 'age' of the information should be carefully noted. Clearly, using data from the 1981 census of population to produce indices of deprivation in 1991 is not likely to produce an accurate reflection of a community. Communities change, land use changes, and the currency of information should always be noted when using information.

Indices

One can use the information collected from secondary sources in a composite way to create an 'index'. Perhaps the most commonly used index in community profiles is an index of deprivation or disadvantage. A recent report uses the 1991 census of population to rank all localities in the UK on both a number of indicators of disadvantage and on an index based on just four such indicators.[15] A number of similar indices are available and have been used by local authorities and health organizations for a variety of uses, including resource allocation, policy review, targetting services and developing bids for resources.[16] The main problems in constructing such indices are disagreement about what 'indicators' are good measures of deprivation and the limitations of available secondary statistics in terms of geographical coverage, frequency, comparability and access. Traditionally, the census of population has been used to create these indicators and, consequently, they are nearly always outdated. One of the most commonly used indicators is the 'Jarman Underprivileged Area Score' or Jarman Index.[17]

Such indices of deprivation/disadvantage[18] have been criticized on a number of grounds. First, many indicators used in their construction do not distinguish between the measurement of deprivation and the kind of people experiencing the deprivation. For example, age, ethnicity and single parenthood are often used indicators in constructing indices, yet they are not *causes* of deprivation even though people in these groups are at greater risk of being disadvantaged. Second, as Townsend has noted, there is a distinction between material and social deprivation. He has defined thirteen types of deprivation using seventy-seven indicators which he divides into material deprivation and social deprivation.[19] Material deprivation includes: dietary, clothing, housing, home facilities, environment, location and work. Social deprivation includes: rights to employment, family activities, integration into the community, formal participation in social institutions, recreation and education. In operational terms, however, due to statistical limitations, he uses just four census indicators to create an index of material deprivation: unemployment, overcrowding, not owning a car and not owning a home.

Third, are the indicators used valid? Do they measure what they mean to measure? Indicators are only surrogates, proxies for possibly unmeasurable phenomena. For example, the census of population results for households lacking two basic amenities, such as exclusive use of a bath or WC, are supposed to 'represent' poor housing. But can these data be used to indicate areas of poor-quality housing? A condemned tower block with damp, asbestos-ridden flats will not show up as poor housing using this indicator if all flats have exclusive facilities.

Key issues

There is a great deal of information already available. Some of it can be used to good effect in producing a community profile provided you are selective in your choice of information and aware of its limitations. Once you have decided what information will be of use to you, how much time and resources you can afford to utilize in collecting the information, you will then have to go in search of it. This chapter should have provided you with a guide to many local sources and your local library may be able to add to this list.

Having obtained this information, you will then have to interpret it, adapt it to your particular purposes and use it to good effect. This might include using it to identify the community to be profiled, checking the representativeness of a survey sample, providing context and comparisons and providing vivid illustration. However, it is highly unlikely that secondary data sources will provide you with all the information you require for your community profile and that you will have to collect some 'new' information yourselves. How you might go about doing this is described in the next two chapters.

Further reading

Beal, C. (1985) *Community Profiling for Librarians*. CRUS Occasional Paper No. 12. Sheffield: University of Sheffield, Centre for Research on User Studies.

Burton, P. (1993) *Community Profiling: Resource and Information Pack* Bristol: University of Bristol, School of Advanced Urban Studies.

Dale, A. and Marsh, C. (eds) (1993) *The 1991 Census Users Guide*. London: HMSO.

Healey, M. (1991) 'The information base: Nature, changes and recommendations for improvement'. In *Economic Activity and Land Use* (M. Healey, ed.) London: Longman.

Huff, D. (1973) *How to Lie with Statistics*. Harmondsworth: Pelican.

Irvine, J. *et al.* (eds) (1979) *Demystifying Social Statistics*. London: Pluto Press.

Notes

1. Lutz, W. (1983) *Using Available Information*, p. 10. Geneva: International Epidemiological Association.
2. Beal, C. (1985) *Community Profiling for Librarians*, p. 213. CRUS Occasional Paper No. 12. Sheffield: University of Sheffield, Centre for Research on User Studies.
3. Op. cit., note 1, p. 40.
4. Brady, S. and Hughes, G. (1991) *Seacroft Sounds Out: A Community Profile*. Leeds: Policy Research Unit.
5. Chapman, M. (1986) *Plain Figures*, p. 9. London: HMSO.
6. *Social Trends*. London: HMSO. Annual.
7. *Regional Trends*. London: HMSO. Annual.
8. These should be available via a local library. Alternatively, HMSO has a number of bookshops and agents who sell their publications. In addition, any good bookshop will be able to order HMSO publications.
9. Census Customer Services, OPCS, Segensworth Road, Titchfield, Hampshire PO15 5RR (tel. 0329 813800).
10. NOMIS, Unit 3P, Mountjoy Research Centre, University of Durham, Durham DH1 3SW (tel. 091 3742468).
11. 'Ministers face exam list uproar', and 'First the facts then their meaning', *Guardian*, 19 November 1992.
12. Healey, M. (1991) 'The information base: Nature, changes and recommendations'. In *Economic Activity and Land Use* (M. Healey, ed.), p. 21. London: Longman.
13. Ibid., p. 22.
14. Huff, D. (1973) *How to Lie with Statistics*. Harmondsworth: Pelican.

15. *People and Places – A 1991 Census Atlas of England* (University of Bristol, School of Advanced Urban Studies 1993).
16. Smith, A. (1993) 'Review of local plans for poverty analysis'. Paper presented at *LARIA Workshop: Census Small Area Indicators of Poverty and Deprivation*, Manchester, 4 February.
17. Jarman, B. (1983) 'Identification of underprivileged areas', *British Medical Journal*, Vol. 286, pp. 1705–1709.
18. A summary of indicators of deprivation is included in: Whitehead, M. (1988) 'The health divide'. In *Inequalities in Health: The Black Report and the Health Divide*, pp. 309–311. Harmondsworth: Penguin.
19. Townsend, P. (1987) *Poverty and Labour in London: Interim Report of a Centenary Study*, pp. 85–94. Survey of Londoners' Living Standards No. 1. London: Low Pay Unit.

5

Collecting new information

Introduction

Community profiles can be compiled on the basis of data collected from the kind of secondary sources described in the previous chapter. Analysis of census data, for example, can give a clear, if limited, picture of an area. However, it is likely that in most cases you will not be able to get all the information you need from existing sources and that you will decide to collect new or primary data. In this and the following two chapters, we examine many of the techniques used in the process of collecting and analysing primary data.

In this chapter, we will look at the range of primary information that might be collected in a community-profiling exercise, the principal methods for collecting it and the strengths and weaknesses of those techniques. We then look at the issues involved in deciding which method is best suited to your particular community profile.

Types of information

Much of what has been said about the collection of secondary data also applies to the collection of original information. Collecting it is time-consuming, skilled work and can be costly. It is essential, therefore, that considerable thought should be given to exactly what information is needed to suit the aims and objectives of your profile.

It is also important to remember the distinction between data that are qualitative (that is, views, opinions, beliefs and attitudes of individuals or groups of people) and data that are quantitative (that is, statistical information that can be used to generalize about the whole, or sections of, the community). Different methods may be used in the collection of these two classes of data, as we shall see. It is essential to be clear about which type of information is required.

In considering what kind of information to collect, you will need to go back to your aims and objectives. Most community profiles are likely to require all or some of the following:

- contextual or background information;
- detailed description of the community and its resources;
- details of the needs of the community;
- existing policies and alternative strategies for the community.

We will discuss each of these in turn.

Contextual information

Contextual information includes general, descriptive and background information that can give a general feel for the community and enables the reader of the final profile to picture the setting clearly in his or her mind. Information in this category will be anything that gives a wide-angled or broad-brush view. This information will be of use both in the introductory chapter of a written profile and will also provide the necessary overview to guide your next steps in undertaking the profile. You will already have collected a great deal of contextual information from a range of secondary sources as described in the previous chapter. This can now be added to.

If the community is a geographically defined one that is new to you, it is worth noting your first impressions of the area. If you know the area well, try and find someone else who does not who is willing to write down their impressions of the area. These might cover such issues as: What is the overall geography of the area like? Are there any natural boundaries? Is it urban or rural? Compact or spread-out? Hilly or flat? Isolated or close to other centres of population? Are the buildings predominantly housing or does the area include industrial or retail estates? What are the houses like? High-rise or low-rise? Well spaced out or compact? And so on. Aerial photographs and large-scale maps can also be helpful in getting a feel for the character of an area. The local library or planning department might be able to help you get hold of maps and aerial photos.

Historical information can also throw light on how the community has developed and changed. This might include both written information (documents, archives, newspapers and old maps), which can be obtained from the local library or local history group, and oral histories (memories, family traditions and local legends), which can be obtained by talking to people, especially older people.

Detailed description of the community and its resources

Having got some general impressions and background information about the community, you will now have to consider how to collect more detailed data about the characteristics of the community and its resources. It is important that these data are comprehensive in their scope and collected systematically. Figure 5.1 gives a checklist of issues about which you might want to collect information and these are discussed in more detail below. Of course, some of this information will already exist and so the methods needed to obtain it will be those discussed in the previous chapter in relation to secondary information.

In considering *land use*, the types of information that you may

Figure 5.1 Community resources

- *Land*: what it is used for; areas that are unused or derelict
- *Environment*: condition of public and private spaces; extent of air, water, noise pollution; roads, railways, footpaths
- *Population*: size; characteristics – age, ethnic composition, employment; status, household composition; etc.
- *Housing*: type, size and tenure of property; standard of repair; house prices/rent levels
- *Local economy*: types of industry and occupation; extent of employment/unemployment
- *Services*: statutory (e.g. education, health, welfare, benefits, etc.); voluntary (e.g. self-help groups, housing associations, social groups, etc.); private sector (e.g. banks, shops, repair services, pubs, cinemas, cafes, garages, etc.)
- *Transport*: buses, trains, etc.
- *Communications*: newspapers, local radio and television, newsletters
- *Power structures*: elected representatives, key groups or activists

want to collect are likely to include: the proportion of the total area given over to different uses such as recreational, accommodation, agricultural, retailing; the relationship between residential, industrial, recreational and other areas; areas or buildings that are unused or derelict; the design and lay-out of streets and estates; and the density of population.

Following on from a consideration of how land is used, you may want to examine the quality of the natural and built environment, including such things as the condition of public areas, buildings and streets; the condition of private gardens, shop fronts and industrial sites; the quality of air and water and the extent of pollution from industry, vehicles and agriculture; noise pollution from aircraft and traffic; the usage, flows and safety of roads and railways; the condition of public footpaths; and the quality of lighting of public areas.

A major focus of attention will inevitably be the *population* of your chosen community. You will almost certainly require information on the size of the population and its composition in terms of age, gender, ethnicity and employment status. In addition, you will probably want the kinds of information that is collected during the census of population, which we discussed in Chapter 4. Some information on *housing* – tenure, type and size or property, level of amenities – will also be available from the census. In addition, you will probably want some information on rents and house prices, standard of repair of houses, local authority waiting lists, homelessness, rent arrears and mortgage repossessions.

The *local economy* is a convenient way of referring to a range of different resources. These include the types of industry that are prevalent in the area; the range of employment these industries provide; and the skills and qualifications of the labour force.

Local services are provided by a range of different organizations – statutory, voluntary and private sector. Some organizations may have offices or workers located within the community; many more will serve the area but not have a daily presence. In collecting information about local services, the kinds of issues that you might address include: the nature, extent and quality of the services provided, including special provision for the disabled; and the structure, catchment area, aims and policies of the organization.

Statutory bodies include organizations such as the local authority, central government departments and agencies such as the TECs, health authority or trust, police and emergency services. They provide, or are responsible for, a wide range of different services such as: schools; community and youth centres; social services such as home helps, social workers, residential care, day centres and advice offices; houses and estate caretakers; sports centres, swimming baths, parks, libraries, art galleries and other cultural and recreational facilities; cemeteries, refuse collection and disposal sites; economic advice; social security offices and job centres; health care facilities such as GPs, health centres, clinics, hospitals and community health practitioners; public transport; police, fire and ambulance services; vocational guidance, careers advice and training provision. The list of services provided by statutory agencies might prove to be very long. It is important to decide in advance which services are particularly relevant to your profile.

Statutory bodies are not the only organizations which provide services to a community. In addition, there is likely to be a number of voluntary organizations which provide services to the community. These might include churches and temples, which are often the focus for a number of community activities such as mother and toddler groups, elderly people's lunch clubs and youth clubs. In addition, self-help groups and campaigning associations often provide services, as do the larger voluntary agencies such as the Council for Voluntary Services, Age Concern, Mind and Shelter. Housing associations are also becoming more important providers of rented housing. Once again the range of voluntary organizations and the extent of services provided will vary enormously between communities and you may need to be selective in the information that you collect.

Some of the most widely used services in any community are likely to be provided by the private sector in the shape of shops, banks, pubs, cafes, restaurants, garages and cinemas. The kinds of issues you might want to consider in relation to these kinds of services include the range of services available, their accessibility and the quality and price of products.

Some resources such as *transport* are likely to be provided by a variety of different kinds of agency. For example, a community is likely to be served by all or some of the following: railways; roads, including motorways; bus services provided by a number of different companies, including perhaps community organizations; trams; underground; and taxis. In collecting information about transport services, the aim will be to assess the adequacy of the services provided for the community being studied, the quality of the service, the cost of using it and whether it is accessible to all sections of the community.

An effective system of *communications* is an important resource which, again, is likely to be provided in a variety of different ways ranging from informal contacts, notices on public display boards, community newsletters and church magazines, local newspapers, radio and television.

Finally, your inventory of community resources would not be complete without some account of the *power structure* which exists within the community. Identifying the bases and structures of power within a community may not be easy, as power can be exercised openly and formally through, for example, elected representatives, or informally through, for example, pressure group activity, a media campaign, or closed meetings between decision makers and those with the ability to make them listen. In considering the power structures that exist within your community, you will need to address the following issues: What is the role and influence of elected representatives such as ward councillors, MPs, Euro MPs, and others on local boards such as school governors? Where are the important decisions made which affect the community? Who is involved in these decision-making processes? Are there influential community groups or key activists who speak for or even dominate all, or sections of, the community? What are the sources of their power?

The needs of the community

A major component of your community profile is likely to be an account of the needs of the community. As we saw in Chapter 1, the concept of need has been the focus for considerable debate. However, in practice, much of this debate has focused not on what people need but on how those needs should be met. It may be useful to separate out these two aspects for the purpose of assessing the needs of the community as part of a community-profiling project. For example, most people would agree that in order to thrive people need nutritious food, clean water, shelter, education and so on. The way in which these needs are satisfied may prove to be more contentious and relate to the social, cultural and economic context of the community whose needs are being assessed. In thinking about the needs of a community, it might be useful to construct

Figure 5.2   Intermediate needs

- Adequate nutritional food and water
- Adequate protective housing
- A non-hazardous work environment
- A non-hazardous physical environment
- Appropriate health care
- Security in childhood
- Significant primary relationships
- Physical security
- Economic security
- Safe birth control and child-bearing
- Basic education

a list of all the things that contribute to people's well-being.[1] A useful starting point in drawing up such a list is the set of basic and intermediate needs identified by Doyal and Gough.[2] They argue that all human beings have basic needs for health and autonomy, the achievement of which require the satisfaction of a set of intermediate needs as shown in Fig. 5.2.

For each of the needs which you identify, it should be possible to state what information you require to determine the level at which that need is currently being met. Clearly, some of these intermediate needs (e.g. basic education), are easier to obtain information about than others (e.g. security in childhood). Nevertheless, even with the less tangible needs it may be possible to collect information that sheds some light on the level of need satisfaction.

When identifying needs, however, it is important not to stress just the negative aspects of a community leaving readers with a poor image of the community as a whole. Most communities have strengths as well as needs and these also deserve to be mentioned.

Existing and alternative policies

The information on needs and resources within the community should allow you to identify those needs which are already being met and services and resources which are already available to the community. It should also allow you to specify those areas where there is a shortfall between needs on the one hand and resources on the other, and other issues which require action to be taken. You might then want to go on to examine the plans and policies that agencies active in the community have for the future. Analysing secondary sources of information as described in the last chapter is a good starting point; however, policies are not always formally stated or documented and may need to be teased out. Interviewing key elected representatives, chairs of committees and officers can produce detailed information on plans and policies. The process of developing action plans and alternative strategies for the community is usually undertaken after the community profile has been completed and we will therefore look at this in more depth in Chapter 9.

Methods for collecting information

Having decided what information you need to collect in relation to resources, needs and existing policies and alternative strategies, you must now decide how to go about collecting it. Whichever method you decide to use there are two primary considerations that should inform all your methods of collecting data:

- be specific and systematic; and
- be objective.

It is essential that you collect information as carefully as possible. Failure to do so can invalidate the information collected and can discredit the whole profile in the eyes of those who are to make use of it, or be persuaded by the results. In the same way, it is vital that the views and opinions of those collecting the data do not interfere with the process. This must be kept in mind, especially when designing any questionnaire, asking questions, leading discussions, or interpreting what is being observed.

In this section, we describe the principal methods you can use in gathering primary data. The two main techniques of relevance to community profiling are *surveys* and *observation*. Surveys are one of the most common methods used for collecting information from a large number of people. They involve people answering a standard set of questions which allows comparisons to be made between groups and statistical and other kinds of analysis to be carried out on the responses. There are two principal ways of conducting a survey: either the respondent (the person answering the questions) answers the questions him/herself, or someone else (the interviewer) asks the questions and records the answers. Surveys are of particular use for collecting information from a large number of people about people. Much of the information about community needs, use of community resources, satisfaction with service delivery and views and attitudes about issues of relevance to the community can be collected by means of a survey. Surveys are also a good way of involving people in the community-profiling process. Surveys are, however, resource-intensive and they require some special knowledge if they are to be carried out in such a way that they produce useful information. For that reason, we will discuss what is involved in doing survey research in detail in the next chapter.

Observation

Not all the information that you require need be collected by means of a survey. Another useful method of obtaining detailed information about the community is through looking, listening and recording in a systematic manner.[3]

Information on the physical aspects of a geographically defined community can be collected through observation. This might include such issues as land use, the condition of housing, road use, and shops and services available within the community. You can also observe the behaviour of people in public places, which can provide insight into how people experience their community and the difficulties they may encounter in day-to-day life. For example, you might want to observe where people cross the road, where children play, the places where young people congregate and so on. You can also use observation to provide insight into the ways in which members of a community interact with each other, for example at community group meetings or places where people come together informally, such as parent and toddler groups or elderly people's lunch clubs. Observing the meetings of community groups and public meetings convened regarding specific topics can provide valuable information about the everyday concerns of members of the community.

Information on the way in which services are delivered to the community can also be gained from observation. How long do people have to wait to be seen in the benefit office? How are tenants treated in the local housing office? Do the refuse people take away all the rubbish? What times of the day do people make most use of the local library?

Much of the information that is obtained through this type of observation exercise will not be amenable to statistical analysis. However, it can provide you with useful insights into the life of the community. Observation also allows you to gather information about groups of people who it is difficult to involve in surveys, such as children who abuse solvents. Observation might provide answers to questions such as: Where do they go? Why do they do it? How many are involved?

Some situations, by their very nature, can only be observed once because they are unique events such as a community group meeting. However, it is also possible to observe some events in the community over time. In the same way that surveys can be repeated to identify any changes that might have occurred, so it is possible to repeat an observation exercise to see whether any changes have resulted following a new policy initiative. For example, how many stray dogs are there in a community spotted before and after a local campaign of canine awareness?

Techniques of observation

There are essentially two approaches to observation – direct observation and participant observation – reflecting the level of involvement one has with the people or groups under observation. *Direct observation* allows the researcher to examine the community without his or her presence influencing the behaviour of those being observed; in other words, the aim is to simply watch what is going on without taking any part in the activities. However, this can be quite difficult to achieve. The presence of a researcher at a community group meeting may affect the way in which group members interact with each other. Also, an outsider may misinterpret the meaning of people's actions and behaviour. For example, does the presence of large numbers of people at the local church indicate high levels of religious belief or is it simply the best place for people to meet their neighbours?

Participant observation allows you to understand better the meaning and motives for people's actions and behaviour. Participant observers do not simply watch what is going on but become involved in the group that they are observing. So a researcher undertaking a participant observer study of a community would not just go along to a parent and toddler group and watch what went on there, but would take his or her own toddler and become an active participant. Obviously, this kind of involvement requires a much longer time-scale, as the researcher must build up trust with the groups that they are wishing to observe. There is also the danger that they may become too involved in what it is they are trying to observe. An outsider may be in a better position to see things that those more closely involved take for granted. A participant observer may become so involved that it becomes very difficult to record events and interpersonal interactions objectively.

Another way of thinking about observation is in terms of the level of conspicuousness of the observer. Here the choice is between *overt observation* and *covert observation*. In the former the observer will explain his or her presence and the purpose of the research, and in the latter those being observed will be unaware that they are being observed. We have already stated that the conspicuous presence of an observer may alter or influence the behaviour of those being observed. A police officer recording the speeds of vehicles in a side street, for example, may well have the effect of slowing many drivers down a little. This may suggest the need for covert observation. However, there are practical difficulties associated with covert observation, such as not being able to take notes at the time. There are also ethical issues that need to be addressed, such as confidentiality and breaking people's trust in your assumed identity.

Whichever technique of observation you use, it is important to try to retain objectivity and to record faithfully what you observe. We all see and experience our surroundings and each other constantly; however, that does not mean we observe objectively all that happens. We are usually highly selective in assimilating and translating the vast array of information that reaches our brain through our various senses. Observing the community in this unstructured way can give valuable information and impressions that can be built on using other methods. However, it is important to recognize the kinds of subconscious selections you are making and what you may be missing. It may help, therefore, if you observe in a structured way, having decided beforehand what you want to observe under a series of categories and recording your observations under these headings.

So far we have indicated a number of ways that you might go about observing the community: standing on street corners with a notepad and pen; spending a day or more in the community centre; joining the local social club; or standing in the queue outside the post office on a Thursday morning. Observation can also include

Figure 5.3 Using video

Going out into a community with a video camera can encourage
people to express their views and opinions about their community.
You can also capture events graphically as they happen. Films of
packs of dogs, children playing in unsuitable sites, people crossing
busy roads and damp peeling wallpaper, can all give weight and
colour to your community profile.

With a little knowledge and skill you can edit the tapes to produce
a strong graphic record of those views and events. However, to
produce a good video can be very time-consuming and costly.

the use of measuring instruments and techniques to record objectively the subject you are observing. There are also a number
of other techniques that we and others have found useful when
undertaking community profiles, which are described in Figs
5.3–5.6.

Figure 5.4 Using a street map

In the 1970s, a technique was devised by community workers to help
them to understand the issues of importance to a community. The
researcher would stand in a busy street, looking puzzled or lost, with
a map in hand and stop to talk to passers-by. This can lead to many
interesting discussions about the area, the environment and its in-
habitants, and produce insights that are less easily obtained using
more formal methods.

Figure 5.5 Community walk

The community walk is a useful way of getting to know a community. Those involved in the profile may want to simply walk
around an area making notes and discussing what they see. This can
bring a number of benefits. A clearer picture of the community may
emerge; issues may be seen more clearly and in context; ideas and
opportunities for further research may present themselves. It also has
the added benefit that encounters with local people may provide
opportunities to explain what the profiling exercise is for.

Figure 5.6   Use of measuring and recording instruments

There are many devices that can assist in the process of objectively measuring and recording your observations. You may wish to add to the following list:

- *Recording*: camera, video, tape-recorder
- *Measuring*: damp meter, thermometer, noise meter, pedometer, map and ruler, stopwatch, automatic counter, chemical analysis of polluted water, soil, etc.

Combining information-gathering techniques

Different methods of collecting information have different uses and each has its own advantages and disadvantages. Therefore, if at all possible, it is advisable to include more than one method, combining them in such a way that they complement each other. For example, initial observations and a semi-structured interview of key workers and community activists can help to identify a broad range of issues that are of concern to the community. A survey of a carefully constructed sample will throw more light on the extent of feeling about those issues as well as providing essential details about the characteristics of the population. From the survey, a number of key issues may emerge that need further elaboration by means, perhaps, of a case study or series of group discussions.[4] Also, the techniques for collecting primary data outlined here should be combined with those of gathering secondary information described in the previous chapter. The way in which different methods might be combined are illustrated in the following examples of the use of case studies and service user studies.

Case studies

A case study is an in-depth examination of one example or instance of a wider phenomenon which makes use of a variety of different methods of enquiry.[5] For example, a survey of a community may show that isolation is a particular problem experienced by older people in that community. You could then use a case study approach to highlight that issue. This might entail an in-depth interview with one or more older people focusing on the issue of social contact and isolation; interviews with a local GP and social worker to discuss the implications of social isolation for health and well-being; and discussions with appropriate groups about how the issue might be tackled.

Case studies allow the researcher to go beyond the initial identification of issues and provide an elaboration of what those issues mean for individuals within the community. Case studies also add colour and life to a community profile.

Service user studies

Service user studies are another possible element of a community profile that makes use of a variety of different techniques of data collection. For example, if you are looking at the usage of a community centre, you might start by analysing existing information such as committee minutes, newsletters, annual reports and records of bar profits. You could then conduct a survey of users of the community centre and interview staff, committee members and user group leaders. You may also wish to have a group discussion with existing user groups in order to identify problems, potentials and issues. You could also use observation techniques to record what actually happens in the building throughout the course of a typical day noting, for example, the length of time people spend in certain parts of the building, the facilities they use and people they contact.[6]

Deciding on the appropriate technique

In Chapter 2, we discussed the importance of making decisions about data collection methods that reflect the kind of information required and the aims, objectives and ultimate purpose of the community profile. In this chapter, we have suggested that where possible it is a good idea to make use of a range of different methods so that you end up with different kinds of information. Nevertheless, you will still have to make decisions about which techniques to use bearing in mind the time and resources you have at your disposal.

In making those decisions, you will need to address the following questions: Who is to be included in the community to be profiled? What is the scope of the profile to be? What kind of data do you need? What practical considerations do you need to take account of? Your answers to the question of who is to be included in the community to be profiled should include the size of the community,

the groups of people involved and whether you are including community representatives, groups and service providers. All of these
issues will influence your choice of information-gathering technique. For example, the size of the population will tell you whether
it is possible to undertake a series of in-depth interviews or a postal
survey. Knowledge of your community will also rule out some
types of information-gathering technique. Some groups are unlikely
to respond to requests for interviews; others may be unwilling to
participate in group discussions. It may not be possible to get access
to certain groups for the purpose of observation.

Your decisions about the scope of the profiling project will tell
you whether you need to focus on the community's perceptions of
their own needs, which might perhaps entail a survey or others'
perceptions of the needs of the community, which might be gleaned
from a series of semi-structured interviews. If you want to build
up a picture of resources within the community, you may want to
use a community walk or mapping exercise. The identification of
the strengths of the community might entail a variety of different
techniques, including interviews, oral histories and analysis of
documentary evidence.

What kind of information do you need? Is the aim of the profile
to produce a report that is intended to persuade someone else of
a particular argument, for example that the community does not
receive an adequate level of resources or needs extra services or
facilities? If so, what kind of information will be most persuasive?
Valid statistical data are often the most difficult to argue with. If
this is what you want, then you will have to select information-
gathering techniques which are appropriate to statistical analysis
and manipulation such as surveys. Observation techniques may
also allow you to produce statistical information, for example the
total number of occurrences of a particular event in a specified time
period. However, not everyone will be persuaded by rather dry
statistical information. Some are more likely to be affected by a
detailed case study, verbatim comments drawn from unstructured
interviews or group discussions or detailed observations.

What are the practical considerations that you need to take
account of in deciding on the methods to use? The time-scale for
completion is one issue. Some methods, such as participant
observer studies or large-scale surveys, take much longer than
others, such as a series of group discussions. The resources you
have available for undertaking the community profile is another

issue. It is easy to underestimate the resources that are needed to tackle some of the techniques we have described. For example, the resources needed for a large-scale postal survey will include printing the questionnaire, covering letter and reminder, envelopes and postage and use of a computer. Similarly, analysis of survey data will require computing skills.

Key issues

Information is the foundation of a community profile, whether it takes the form of statistics, opinions, beliefs, traditions, pictures or even poetry. The quality of the information, together with the way in which it is presented, will largely determine whether people find the profile interesting, relevant, useful, startling or just informative. Therefore, you need to give considerable thought to what information you need and how it is to be gathered.

In Chapter 4, we looked at what is entailed in collecting secondary information. In this chapter, we have described some of the techniques for collecting primary information. The types of primary information that you might require include contextual or background information, detailed information about the community and its services and resources, the needs of the community and information about existing policies and alternative strategies. These categories of information can be collected using a variety of different methods, although the principal ones are surveys and observation. In deciding which methods to use, it is important that you are clear about what information is required and why, and that you take account of the practical considerations which will affect your choice and to be realistic about what you can manage.

Further reading

Bell, J. (1993) *Doing Your Research Project*, 2nd edn. Buckingham: Open University Press.

Gilbert, N. (ed.) (1993) *Researching Social Life*. London: Sage.

Kane, E. (1991) *Doing Your Own Research*. London: Marion Boyars.

Kingsley, S. and Taylor, M. (1985) *Research in Voluntary and Community Organisations: Some Guidelines for Employing Researchers*. Wivenhoe: ARVAC.

de Vaus, D.A. (1991) *Surveys in Social Research*. London: Allen and Unwin.

Walker, R. (ed.) (1985) *Applied Quantitative Research*. London: Gower.

Notes

1. For a discussion of this type of approach, see Percy-Smith, J. and Sanderson, I. (1991) *Understanding Local Needs*. London: Institute for Public Policy Research.
2. Doyal, L. and Gough, I. (1991) *A Theory of Human Need*. London: Macmillan (summarized on p. 170).
3. Many of the profiles in our Bibliography have used observation techniques. Some that may by worth examining include: *Bloomsbury Safety Audit* (Safer Estates for Women 1992); *A Photographic Memory* (Hulme 1986); *Communities Under the Hammer: Privy to Privatization* (Griffiths *et al.* 1988); *The Cry of the People of Buttershaw* (Shiner 1991); and *A Short Study of the Neighbourhood Areas of Rhyl and Communities Under Stress* (Devonshire 1984).
4. Many of the profiles that we have examined used a combination of techniques, including *Bloomsbury Safety Audit* (Safer Estates for Women 1992) and *Thorntree Ward Survey* (Community Economy Ltd 1989).
5. Newcastle City Council undertook a case study as part of its *Newcastle Upon Tyne – A Social Audit* (1985).
6. In *Pembury: The Library and the Community* (1981), Cathy Hamblin describes a service user study which she undertook into the library service along similar lines to those in our example here.

6

Survey methods

Introduction

Although surveys are not the only way of collecting new information from a community (see Chapter 5), they are one of the most important methods of collecting accurate information from a representative sample of the community that will enable you to make general statements about that community with any degree of confidence. Data from surveys can often be persuasive, which may be important if you are trying to convince someone else of a particular argument. However, information from surveys is only as good as the tools that were used to collect that information. This is an area where it is very easy to make mistakes that can invalidate almost all of the information collected by your survey. Given that surveys are costly to undertake in terms of both money and people resources, you should be quite sure that you really need to do a survey to collect the information you require and if the answer to this is 'yes', that you have in your group, or have access to, skills and expertise in relation to survey design. If you have sufficient resources but insufficient expertise and that expertise is not available from elsewhere (for example, your local university or college), then you may want to consider using a relatively small amount of resources to buy in some professional expertise and assistance on survey design and analysis (see Chapter 2).

In this chapter, we will examine the various kinds of survey methods available and review their advantages and disadvantages in different situations. We will then move on to look at samples and sampling, how to design a questionnaire or interview schedule and recruitment and training of interviewers. This chapter focuses on survey methods for community profiles; we work on a 'need-to-know' basis, providing the information on survey methods that is necessary for anyone embarking on a survey for a community profile. The chapter is not intended as a detailed review of survey research methods as such. Anyone requiring a more in-depth analysis should turn to any of the specialist texts indicated in the further reading at the end of the chapter.

Survey methods: Advantages and disadvantages

In essence, a survey is a way of collecting information in a standard format from a relatively large number of people. Collecting information in a structured way is necessary if you want to be able to analyse that information relatively easily (especially important if you are using a computer) and also if you want to be able to compare the responses of different groups of people. Surveys can be divided into those which require respondents (those persons answering the questions) to complete the survey questionnaire themselves (self-completion questionnaires) and those which require that someone else asks the questions (interview surveys).

Self-completion surveys

Self-completion surveys are usually posted or delivered to people's homes. Postal surveys, in particular, can be relatively quick and easy to administer and it is possible to reach quite a lot of people in this way. The disadvantages are that they tend to result in quite low response rates. In other words, the proportion of those receiving a questionnaire who complete and return it may be low. In addition, your response sample (those completing and returning the questionnaire) may not be representative, as certain groups of people are notoriously reluctant to fill in questionnaires of this kind. And, furthermore, it is often those who are most vulnerable, disadvantaged or alienated within a community who are least likely to return questionnaires. Another problem with self-completion questionnaires is that people have to be reasonably literate in order to complete them and, again, this is an assumption that cannot always be made. A further difficulty with self-completion question-naires is that they work best with a relatively small number of 'tick box' questions. This may be problematic if you want to ask more 'open' questions (see below) or want respondents to give a more considered response.

However, some of these difficulties can be overcome. For

example, the response rate can be improved by making the questionnaire attractive and easy to complete. You can also make it easy for people to return their questionnaires, for example by providing a pre-paid, addressed envelope, or by sending people out to collect questionnaires and, perhaps, offer assistance to complete them. In addition, you might want to offer an incentive for completion and return, such as the chance to be entered in a prize draw. Where a community contains significant numbers of people for whom English is not their first language, translations of the questionnaire into the appropriate languages should be made available.

The types of situation in which self-completion questionnaires might be useful are where you want to get a fairly superficial, broad-brush indication of issues from a relatively large group of people. In small communities, especially where those communities are geographically concentrated, then they may be less useful.

Interview surveys

Interview surveys involve one person, the interviewer, talking to another person or persons, the respondent or respondents. They may be structured or semi-structured. A structured interview is based on a standard, prepared questionnaire which the interviewer works through with the respondent. The advantage of this method is that it is easy to compare answers from different people because you have asked them all the same questions. The disadvantage is that it may result in a rather stilted conversation and hence less useful information than might otherwise be the case.

A semi-structured interview could be based around a checklist of questions or issues that you want to cover in the course of the discussion without the precise wording of those issues being formulated in advance. The advantage of this method is that it generally leads to a more informal dialogue, which should mean that the interviewee is more forthcoming. The disadvantage is that it is more difficult to analyse the information, as it will not be in a standard format. Also, it may mean that the interviews take rather a long time. Interviewers conducting semi-structured interviews must be well-briefed or highly knowledgeable about the subject matter under discussion.

Interview surveys are more flexible than self-completion surveys in that they may be structured or semi-structured, involve open or closed questions, may be carried out with individuals or groups, in the street, on the telephone or in people's own homes. They also entail more personal contact, which should create a greater sense of involvement with the project and it is also much easier to ensure that the response sample is representative of the community as a whole. Telephone surveys tend to be more like self-completion surveys in terms of the kinds of questions that can be asked. However, they can be a particularly quick and easy way of reaching a lot of people quite quickly.

The disadvantages are that interview surveys – especially those carried out with individuals – are resource-intensive in terms of people and those people undertaking the interviews will require considerable training. Responses from interviews which include a lot of in-depth or qualitative questions may be difficult to code and analyse. Telephone interviews can be problematic in terms of the response sample in that you can only contact those households with telephones.

Group discussions

Community profiles are often concerned, wholly or partly, with issues which affect both individuals and the community as a collectivity. You may, therefore, want to adopt a more collective approach to gathering information by using group discussions or group interviews. When discussing issues in a group, people can often begin to formulate and articulate views that had previously only been vague ideas, their understanding of issues may be clarified by what others are saying, and new ideas and issues may emerge. However, you will not be able to get quantitative data from group discussions; they can be difficult to analyse; discussion groups are rarely representative, so it is not possible to make generalizations about the community as a whole; and to orchestrate an effective group discussion requires considerable facilitation skills.

Combining survey methods

Rather than using just one of these survey methods, you may want to consider using different methods in combination with each other in order to maximize the advantages and minimize the disadvantages. For example, you could use a fairly short postal questionnaire to get some basic quantitative data, then use individual

Figure 6.1   Issues to consider when deciding on survey methods

- The purpose of the profile
- The aims and objectives of the project
- The type of information you want to collect – quantitative or qualitative, 'facts' or perceptions
- Who you want to obtain information from – individual residents, groups of residents, front-line service providers, community representatives
- The resources you have at your disposal – money, time, people
- The skills that you have within your group – questionnaire design, interviewing skills, computing expertise, data analysis, group work

interviews to target particular groups who you are especially interested in, and then organize a series of group discussions to discuss the findings of the earlier stages of the project and start identifying priorities for action.

In deciding which of these survey techniques to use, you will need to consider the issues listed in Fig. 6.1. So, for example, if the community profile is mainly intended to be part of a broader community development exercise, it may be the case that the process is as important as the information collected, which might suggest the need for survey methods which maximize the opportunities for community participation, for example door-to-door interviewing. If, on the other hand, the aim is to persuade an organization that the community has significant needs which are currently not being met, then methods which result in lots of 'hard' statistical information may be more appropriate, such as a postal survey of a large sample.

Samples and sampling

At the same time as you are considering what kind of survey method to adopt, you will also need to give some thought to your sample. The sample is the group of people who are directly involved in the survey through being interviewed or sent a self-completion questionnaire. As with survey design more generally, sampling is quite a difficult technical exercise and one that is important, since it can affect the validity and reliability of the information that you collect (see Chapter 4). If you ask the 'wrong' people to take part in your survey, then you might end up with information that is not very useful. Again, it is worth seeking assistance from others with particular expertise in this area, although this section should provide you with the basic knowledge to derive a sample.

Your starting point will be the whole community in which you are interested. Having drawn an imaginary line around this community, you must then decide what kinds of people within the community you are interested in talking to. Let's take as an example a spatially defined community such as a housing estate. Are you interested only in the views of those who live on the estate or those who are employed there as well? Are you interested in everyone's views or only those of the adult residents? Are you taking eighteen or sixteen as the age at which people are deemed to be adults?

Having answered these questions and decided on the type of people whose views you are interested in, you must then decide on how many people you can reasonably contact given the survey methods you intend to use, the resources you have at your disposal and the time-scale for completion of the project. Whether you have access to a computer to store and analyse the information that you collect may be an important consideration in deciding how many people to survey (see Chapter 7).

Of course, it may be the case that you want to ask questions of everyone of a particular type of person, for example, all the adult residents of an estate. If so, then you have what is called a 100 per cent sample and you have no need to go any further through the process of deriving a sample. In most cases, unless your community is quite small or your resources quite large, this will not be practical and you will need to find a smaller group of people to survey. In deciding who this sample of people should consist of, you need to bear in mind two issues: the number of people who you want to contact and how representative this group is of the community as a whole. What it means for a sample to be representative is that the characteristics of your sample match as closely as possible those of the community at large. The characteristics which are of particular importance in this regard are gender, age, ethnicity, place of residence and employment status. So, if you know that 25 per cent of the population is aged over sixty-five in your community, then you should try to ensure that your sample contains 25 per cent of people over sixty-five. If you end up with responses from a larger proportion of people over sixty-five, then it is quite likely that the views expressed will be biased and fail to reflect accurately the views of the wider community.

In order to ensure that your sample is representative, you will need some information about the characteristics of the population that makes up the community in which you are interested. In most cases, this can be obtained from census data (see Chapter 4). However, there may be other characteristics which are of importance depending on the purpose of your profile. For example, if your focus is a particular group of people within the population such as elderly people, then it may be important to get a sample that is representative in terms of whether or not they live alone, with relatives or in sheltered accommodation.

Sampling frames

Having decided on the population to be sampled, identified the characteristics of that population and decided how many individuals you want in your sample, you must then obtain a sampling frame. A sampling frame is essentially a comprehensive list of those individuals or organizations relevant to your survey from which you will derive the actual individuals or organizations who will be contacted. It might be the electoral register for a particular area, a list of voluntary or community organizations, a list of ward councillors or a register of users of a particular service. You need to be sure that your sampling frame includes all the people who you are interested in. For example, if you want to include sixteen-year-olds in your sample, then the electoral register will not be much use because only those aged seventeen and above are included. Also, you must be sure that you have excluded from the sampling frame all those who are not relevant. For example, if you are only interested in surveying women, then you must make sure that your sampling frame only contains women. If your sampling frame does not allow you to identify the particular characteristics of individuals in which you are interested, then you may need to identify a larger initial sample and then use some kind of screening mechanism for excluding those who do not fit your criteria (see below).

The electoral register is one of the most widely used sampling frames. The electoral registration office of your local authority will have a register of the names and addresses of all those aged seventeen and over who have registered to vote. The register is organized by polling district and street, so it is quite easy to find the streets that relate to the area you want to profile. However, there are a number of disadvantages associated with drawing your sample from the electoral register; for various reasons, not all those who live in the area will have registered to vote. Often those who are most needy or vulnerable will be precisely those who have not registered. This problem may be further compounded if you choose to use a postal questionnaire (see above). You usually have to pay for the electoral register. The electoral register will not tell you whether people are black or white, employed or unemployed, young or old, so if you want to focus on a particular group in the population then this is a problem. Nevertheless, despite difficulties, it may prove to be the most comprehensive list of adults available.

Having obtained a comprehensive sampling frame, you must now decided on the technique for drawing your sample that is most appropriate to your project. There are three main approaches: random sampling, stratified sampling or quota sampling.

Random sampling

Random sampling is so-called because everyone included in the sampling frame has an equal chance of being selected. However, random in this context does not mean haphazard. For example, it would not be a random sample if you simply walked through the estate interviewing everyone who you happened to encounter. Some residents would be at home or at work or somewhere else and so could not be said to have had an equal chance of being interviewed. Random sampling is a technique with rules that must be adhered to. Nevertheless, it is a fairly simple technique. You can derive a random sample in two ways. The first is to use a set of random number tables which can usually be found at the back of statistics textbooks or you can buy books of random numbers or you can use a computer to generate a random number. Random numbers usually appear as five digits and reading from the left you should use as many of the digits you need in order to identify your sample. So, if there are less than 100 individuals in your sampling frame, use only the first two digits of each random number. If there are between 100 and 999 individuals, use three digits and so on. Simply work through the lists of random numbers either going down the column or up the column or from left to right or right to left, but always consistently. Once you have a set of random numbers equivalent to the number you want to arrive at in your sample, then you can identify the sample by picking out the numbers of those individuals in the sampling frame to match the random numbers.

An easier way to obtain a random sample is to take the number of individuals in the sampling frame and divide it by the number of people who you want to end up with in your sample in order to obtain the sampling interval. Then, using a random number that is less than the total number of individuals in the sampling frame, use the individual in the sampling frame who corresponds to that number as your starting point and use the sampling interval to identify the next name and so on. So if you have a sampling frame of 2000 and you want a sample of 200, then you will have a sampling interval of 10. If the random number tables give you a number of 596, then the individual who appears as 596th on the list will be the first in the sample. Working from here you should then identify every tenth entry on the list going back to the beginning when you reach the last entry, until you have your sample of 200. This method of sampling is very easy to do but cannot be used if there is a bias of any kind in the sampling frame. In other words, if the list groups people in any way, for example by age, then this kind of sampling cannot be used and the more complicated random sampling techniques described above should be employed.

Stratified random sampling

An alternative, slightly more complex approach is to use stratified random sampling. This technique is particularly useful when you want to guarantee that certain sections of the community are included. So, for example, if you have a community that consists of three identifiably different populations, for example a white population, a Pakistani population and an Afro-Caribbean population, you may want to stratify your sample so that it is proportional to these three constituent elements. So if the total population is 5000 and 3000 of these people (or 60 per cent) are white and 1000 (or 20 per cent) are Pakistani and a further 1000 (or 20 per cent) Afro-Caribbean, you would need to ensure that the sample contained appropriate proportions of these three groups. In practice, you would need separate sampling frames for each of the three communities and then randomly sample the appropriate number of individuals from each as described above.

Quota sampling

A third method of sampling is quota sampling. This is similar in some respects to stratified sampling in that the aim is to ensure that the sample reflects certain known characteristics of the population; for example, if you know that 25 per cent of the population is aged over sixty-five, then 25 per cent of the people in your sample should also be over sixty-five. However, quota samples are usually based on more than one characteristic. For example, you may want to take account of gender, age, ethnicity and employment status. The sample that you derive should then ensure that it contains appropriate proportions of people with these characteristics. The important difference here is that the sample is not derived entirely randomly. Rather, the researcher sets out to find appropriate numbers of people with the particular characteristics specified in the quota.

Cluster sampling

There is one other kind of sampling technique, cluster sampling, which may be important if you are taking a community that is widely dispersed, for example women in a particular city or district. This technique actually involves two layers of sampling: the first samples areas of the city or district and the second identifies individuals within those areas. Thus the sample is clustered in that individuals identified in the sample are concentrated in particular parts of the city. This is especially useful when it is not practicable for interviewers to cover a very large geographical area or where it would be too costly or time-consuming to work through a very large sampling frame, for example the entire electoral register for a city.

The first thing to do is to divide the city or district into appropriate areas which can then be sampled. Usually, the easiest way to do this is on the basis of polling districts, census enumeration districts or wards. First, you will need to know the total population for each area. List each area with the cumulative population next to it. Having decided how many areas you want to end up with, divide the total population for all the areas by the number of areas you want in the sample to give the sampling frame. Then, using a random number start, identify the areas by adding the sampling interval and then identifying the area which contains the cumulative population total that contains this figure. The reason for doing this is no matter whether areas have large or small populations, they have an equal chance of being sampled. Alternatively, you may want to ensure that you include a range of different areas within a city or district which display certain characteristics. For example, you may want to ensure that you include rich and poor areas, white and multicultural, areas of owner-occupied housing and council estates. If so, you will need to specify the characteristics precisely, determine which indicators to use, group the areas appropriately and then randomly sample within these groupings. In effect, you are stratifying your sampling points using this method. Having identified the areas or sampling points, it is then possible to identify the sample of individuals using any of the methods described above.

Whichever method you decide to use to derive your sample, you should follow the rules carefully to ensure that the sample that you end up with is as unbiased as possible.

Drafting a questionnaire

Whichever survey method and sampling technique you decide upon, you will have to develop some basic tools to use during the survey. The most important of these is the survey questionnaire, whether it is for self-completion or interview. Before you start drafting your questionnaire, be sure that you can answer the following questions:

- What kinds of information do you need? For information on needs, needs as seen by whom? For information on resources, which resources? Existing, potential or alternative?
- How will the questions be asked? For example, by postal survey, telephone interview, semi-structured group discussion?
- Who will be answering the questions?
- How is the information from the questionnaires to be stored and analysed?
- What are the issues that have been identified during the project so far?

How you answer these questions will determine the kind of questionnaire that you design.

The next step is to try to list all the issues that your questionnaire ought to cover and the kinds of information that you need to collect from the survey. You may find it useful to go back to the issues identified in the 'preparing the ground' stages of the project and also to the project aims and objectives as a starting point. Don't worry at this stage about how you will ask the questions, simply focus on what you need to know. Some issues that you may want to consider are whether you only want to get at 'facts' (e.g. how many people make use of a community centre) or whether you are concerned also about attitudes and opinions (e.g. what users of the community centre think about that facility) and suggestions (e.g. what other uses the community centre could be put to). Other types of question include those which seek to discover the strength of feeling in a community about a particular issue; those which are intended to find out how aware the respondent is of an issue; those which require respondents to rank issues or statements in order of importance to them or to choose between alternatives. You will almost certainly need to get some information on the personal characteristics of those people who are taking part in the survey. This is to enable you to disaggregate the information so that the views of different groups can be compared and contrasted and to check how representative the response sample is of the community as a whole.

Having put together a list of issues, information sought through the questionnaire and types of question, you must now start to think about the layout of your questionnaire. This is especially important for self-completion surveys, as questionnaires that are badly produced and difficult to understand will be off-putting to those completing them. But interview surveys also require well-designed questionnaires that make the task of the interviewer much easier. Figure 6.2 lists some basic rules of questionnaire design. Semi-structured interview surveys usually only require a carefully considered checklist of issues to be discussed.

You now have to make a number of decisions. How long is the questionnaire to be? If it is a postal questionnaire, then the number of pages is probably more important than the length of time it takes to complete. A very long questionnaire arriving through the post is likely to be very off-putting. If it is an interview schedule, then the length of time it takes to do the interview is likely to be more important. For both self-completion and interview surveys, the general rule is to make the questionnaire as short as possible

Figure 6.2   Basic rules about questionnaire design

- Make sure that any instructions are clearly written and easy to follow
- Keep the layout simple with plenty of room for responses
- Use simple language
- Avoid ambiguity
- Make sure that questions follow a logical order
- Avoid asking questions that may cause offence. If you do ask questions about sensitive issues, then try to put them near the end of the questionnaire
- Be consistent in the terms used, e.g. to refer to the local area
- Ask specific rather than general questions

consistent with the kind of information that you are trying to collect.

Having had some initial discussion about these issues, you are now in a position to begin drafting the questionnaire. The front sheet of the questionnaire, or 'face sheet', will usually give the title of the survey and, in the case of self-administered questionnaires, will include instructions on how to complete the questionnaire, what to do with it once it has been completed and an assurance of confidentiality. Interview questionnaires will usually include space on the front sheet to record administrative information, such as the date when the interview was undertaken, the length of the interview and perhaps quota details.

Ordering the questions

Now you must decide on the order in which the issues about which you want to ask questions should appear. In general, it is best to begin with impersonal, easy-to-answer questions which will not challenge or threaten the respondent but will perhaps arouse their interest and secure their cooperation. Try to ensure that the order in which the issues are raised allows a natural flow of ideas. Where you do have to change topic abruptly, you should include a link sentence such as: 'You have just been telling me about the place where you live, now I would like to ask you some questions about employment'.

Open and closed questions

Having decided on the order in which the questions should be asked, you must now think carefully about precisely how to word the questions and what kinds of answers you want. There are basically two kinds of questions to ask – *open* and *closed*. An example of a closed question is as follows:

Please indicate why you like living in this area by ticking the reasons which apply to you:
- ☐ Friendly neighbours
- ☐ Nice houses
- ☐ Good public transport
- ☐ A pleasant environment
- ☐ Quiet roads
  - etc.

This is a closed question because it predetermines the possible reasons that someone might have for liking the area in which they live. An example of an 'open' question is:

Please could you tell me why you like living in this area?

This is open because the respondent can answer in whatever way he or she likes.

There are advantages and disadvantages associated with both open and closed questions. Open questions are much more difficult to code and analyse because there are an almost infinite number of possible responses. In a self-completion questionnaire people are generally more likely not to answer open questions, since they require more effort to answer (and the ability to write), whereas closed questions usually require the respondent simply to tick the appropriate box. Similarly, open questions are more likely to elicit the response 'I don't know', which often means 'I can't be bothered to answer your question or think about the issue'. On the other hand, closed questions may have the effect of imposing the views of the person or group who drafted the questionnaire on those who are responding by effectively dictating the range of possible responses. If you choose to use closed questions, you must at least allow the respondent to say 'I don't know' or have an 'other' category for responses outside your list. The range of answers should be as comprehensive as possible so that people feel that they are being presented with sufficient options.

In an interview survey, it may be better to use show cards for questions with a large number of possible answers. The show card is presented to the respondent when the interviewer reaches that question so that they have all the answer choices in front of them after the interviewer has finished reading them to remind them of the alternatives. If the list is too long, then maybe you should be asking an open question.

The range of possible answers to a closed question should avoid any overlap between categories. For example, if you ask the question 'How old are you?' and the respondent says twenty-five, it is not clear which box the interviewer should tick if the answer categories are as follows:

☐ 16–18
☐ 18–25
☐ 25–35
etc.

In most cases, you will probably want to ask a mixture of open and closed questions and in any case it is often a good idea to vary the ways in which questions are asked so that people are not constantly doing the same thing, such as ticking 'yes' or 'no' or circling a number. When using closed questions, you should make it quite clear to the interviewer or the respondent in self-completion surveys, what they are required to do – tick a box, circle a number, etc. when using open questions, make sure that there is sufficient room for the respondent or the interviewer to write in the answer.

Filter questions

It may be the case that not all questions in the questionnaire will apply to all respondents. If this is the case, you will have to have some mechanism for 'filtering' responses so people are not asked irrelevant questions. One of the most common methods for doing this is to include an instruction immediately following the answer box as follows:

5. Do you have any children? (Tick one)
   Yes ☐ GO TO Q.6
   No ☐ GO TO Q.8

In this example, those respondents with children will then go on to answer question 7, whereas those who do not have children will go straight to question 8. It is important that the instructions attached to filter questions are clear; it is a good idea to use different types for instructions and questions.

Another way of asking a supplementary question following an initial screening question is as follows:

5. Do you have any children under 16 living with you? (Tick one)

      Yes ☐ Please could you write their ages in the boxes.

           1st child ☐ 2nd child ☐ 3rd child ☐
           4th child ☐ 5th child ☐ 6th child ☐

      No ☐

Try to avoid having too many filter questions as they can be confusing. If it seems as if this is going to be the case, you may want to colour-code different sections of the questionnaire which are applicable to different groups of people and have an instruction about which colours are applicable to whom. For example, if you want people to answer different questions according to their employment status, then you could have an instruction along the following lines:

Are you currently:

☐ In paid employment (PLEASE ANSWER QUESTIONS ON BLUE PAGES)

☐ Not in paid work and looking for a job (PLEASE ANSWER QUESTIONS ON GREEN PAGES)

☐ Not in paid work and not looking for work (PLEASE ANSWER QUESTIONS ON PINK PAGES)

Wording of questions

The wording of questions is very important. If you ask a question using inappropriate words, then the respondent may not understand what you are asking and therefore be unable to answer the question. Or, if the question is asked insensitively, then he or she may refuse to answer. In general, the words used and the style in which questions are asked should be familiar to members of the community who will be responding to the questions and comfortable for interviewers to use. It is helpful to pilot your questionnaire in order to uncover difficulties (see below).

There are a number of things to avoid at all costs. These will be discussed briefly in turn.

1. *Leading questions.* These questions encourage the respondent to answer in a particular way. An example of a leading question might be:

> Don't you think this is a friendly neighbourhood? (Tick one)
>   Yes ☐
>   No ☐

A better way of asking about a respondent's assessment of how friendly his or her neighbourhood is might be as follows:

> Please could you tell me how friendly you think this neighbourhood is? (Circle one)
> Very friendly   Fairly friendly
> Not very friendly   Not at all friendly

2. *Vague questions.* These questions include words that are open to different interpretations. An example might be as follows:

> Do you often go to the cinema? (Tick one)
>   Yes ☐
>   No ☐

This is likely to lead to meaningless responses, since what counts as 'often' will vary enormously between individuals. A better way of asking this question might be as follows:

> How often do you go to the cinema? (Tick one)
> ☐ Never
> ☐ At least once a year
> ☐ At least once every six months
> ☐ At least once every three months . . . etc.

3. *Ambiguous terms.* Some commonly used words are too ambiguous to be used without definition. These include: unemployed, housewife, old people, young people, rich, poor and so on. All of these terms will mean different things to different people. In general, it is best to avoid these terms altogether and use more precise words and phrases such as:

- Not currently in paid work for 'Unemployed'.
- Not in paid work and looking after home and family for 'Housewife'.

- Aged 65 or over for 'Old People'.
- Aged 16–21 for 'Young People'.

4. *Hypothetical questions*. These are questions which ask people what they might do in certain hypothetical situations. An example might be:

> If you were to move house, where do you think you would move to?

This type of question is likely to elicit a lot of 'I don't know' responses, since many of those answering the question will not be interested in moving house and will therefore never have given the matter any thought at all. There may, however, be times when it is appropriate to use a hypothetical question, for example if you want to get people to express an ideal or a set of values. You might want to find out what is currently lacking in people's lives by asking a question like:

> If you won £1000, what would you spend it on?

5. *Two questions in one*. These questions are worded in such a way that you are actually asking about two possibly unrelated issues at the same time. For example:

> Do you think that there should be more car parking places or that people should walk to work?

This question is almost impossible to answer as it asks two quite separate questions at the same time.

6. *Questions that are too general*. For example, a question such as:

> What do you think about the houses in this area?

is very difficult to answer. Are you trying to find out about the state of repair of houses, their size, whether they are well-designed, attractive to look at or comfortable to live in? It is far better to ask several more specific questions such as:

> Do you think that the houses in this area are in a good state of repair?
> Would you say that the houses in this area are well-designed?

> etc.

7. *Questions which ask too much*. An example of this type of question might be:

> Please tell me about your last five visits to the doctor, why you went, how easy it was to get an appointment and what was the outcome of your visit?

Far too much is being asked in one question. Again it is far better to ask about each issue in separate questions.

8. *Questions which assume knowledge*. This problem might arise where the language used is technical, or where jargon is included or where abbreviations are used. For example:

> Does your home have uPVC windows?
> Do you think you have become institutionalized as a result of your long stay in hospital?
> How useful do you think NVQs are in finding a job?

Unless you are certain that the people in your sample will understand this kind of technical language or jargon, then avoid using it.

9. *Mental arithmetic questions*. It is not usually a good idea to ask people to do arithmetical calculations, whether it is a self-completion questionnaire or an interview. For example:

> Please could you tell me what your total weekly household income is from all sources, including wages or salary, benefits of all kinds and pensions.

In this case, it would be far better and result in a higher degree of accuracy to list all the possible sources of income and go through them individually and for the interviewer or coder to do the adding up.

10. *Questions that rely on a good memory*. It is unlikely that you will get very accurate responses if you ask people about events too far in the past. For example:

> How many times did you go the local swimming pool over the last year?

In general, the previous six months is a reasonable time-scale about which to ask questions. However, where possible ask about a shorter and more recent time period and, where appropriate, fix it in people's minds by reference to an event such as Christmas.

Piloting the questionnaire

Once you have drafted the questionnaire, you need to test that it actually works. The best way to do this is to try it out on a small group of people who have not been involved in the drafting. This will help you find out whether the questions can be understood and answered appropriately; whether the filter questions work properly; whether the possible answers to your closed questions are sufficiently comprehensive; whether there is enough space to record the answers and so on. During the piloting, the questionnaire should be used in the same way that it will be used in the actual survey. So if it is to be a self-completion questionnaire, then it should be given to those participating in the pilot with no additional information besides the covering letter which would normally accompany the questionnaire (see below). If it is to be an interview, then the interviewer should introduce the questionnaire in the same way that it will be introduced in the survey proper.

Once the pilot questionnaires have been completed, you need to look at the responses and talk to those involved in the pilot – respondents and interviewers – and ask the kinds of questions shown in Fig. 6.3.

Having carried out the pilot and addressed these issues, you should now be in a position to produce the final draft of your questionnaire. Once any amendments arising out of the pilot have been

Figure 6.3   Questions to be considered after the pilot

- Are the types of responses to questions broadly what you expected?
- Can the responses be coded?
- Where some parts of the questionnaire or some questions only apply to certain groups of respondents, do the filtering questions work properly?
- Do any questions seem to have been consistently misinterpreted?
- Do any questions seem redundant?
- Were any questions difficult to ask or to answer?
- Did questions involving show cards work okay?
- Did any of the categories in pre-coded questions seem redundant?
- Did a lot of closed questions elicit responses that fell in to the 'other' category?
- How long did it take to complete the questionnaire?

incorporated, it will need to be proof-read and the numbering checked (especially where questions have been reordered or taken out or added). Survey questionnaires should always be typed or word-processed. Now it is ready to be printed or photocopied.

Distribution and return of self-completion questionnaires

If your survey is a self-completion survey, you will have to arrange for the questionnaires to be delivered to the people identified in your sample. Essentially, there are three ways to do this: post them, deliver them by hand or personally give them to the individuals concerned. Whichever method you choose to employ, you must be certain that you know who the questionnaires have been delivered to and which of them has been returned to you. You must also check that when the questionnaires are delivered to the sample that they know what they are supposed to do with them and why they have received them.

If the questionnaires are delivered by post or by hand, then they will need to be clearly addressed to the person who you want to complete the questionnaire. Where you do not have a named individual to send the questionnaire to, then you will have to address it to 'The Occupier' or 'The Resident'. You will then need to state clearly in the covering letter and on the questionnaire itself who within the household you want to complete the questionnaire. However the questionnaire is delivered it should be accompanied by a letter or leaflet explaining what the survey is about, how to complete the questionnaire, what to do with it when it is completed and what will happen next. The accompanying letter or leaflet should also give an assurance of confidentiality.

If you want respondents to return their questionnaires to you by post, then you will have to include a pre-paid, addressed envelope of an appropriate size when the questionnaire is sent out. Alternatively, you may want to increase the response rate by calling on people and asking them to give you their completed questionnaire or, if they have not yet completed it, ask them if they require any help to do so. This is especially useful in areas where you suspect that poor literacy may affect the response. If you decide to use this method of returning the questionnaires, then you should make it clear in the covering letter accompanying the questionnaire that someone will be calling on them and indicate the approximate time-scale between delivery and collection of the questionnaire. You should still include an envelope with the questionnaire, as some people may feel uncomfortable handing you a form which contains personal information about themselves or their household, especially where those collecting the questionnaires are local volunteers. Of course, you may decide to use pre-paid envelopes for the bulk of responses and only call on those who have not responded within a certain time. This has the advantage of maximizing the amount of time available for chasing up those who might otherwise not respond. If you want to do the whole survey entirely by post, you may instead want to send a reminder letter to those who have not returned their questionnaire to you within a specified time.

Another method of returning questionnaires is to get people to hand them in to a particular place, for example a community centre. However, this is the most demanding way of getting questionnaires returned, since it requires the most effort on the part of the respondent. As a consequence, it may result in a lower response rate than would otherwise be the case.

Logging responses

Whichever method you decide to use to get the questionnaires back, you will need to be able to keep a record of which ones have been returned. This is especially important if you are intending to follow up non-respondents. The simplest way to do this is to give each person or household in your sample an identification number which is written on the questionnaire and also against the name and address of the individual concerned. As questionnaires are returned, you can then simply tick them off so that those who have not yet responded can be easily identified. If you are using a computer to log responses, it is very important that the file containing the names and addresses of individuals in your sample is separate from the data relating to them (see Chapter 7).

You may also want to keep an eye on response rates from particular groups within your overall sample, so that you can identify especially low responses in certain quarters at an early stage and take appropriate action (e.g. reminder letters, visits, etc.) to boost the response from such groups. If you are to do this, then you will need to have some basic information on the characteristics of the population (see above) to enable you to assess whether response rates are particularly low or high.

Recruitment and training of interviewers

If you are undertaking an interview survey, then you will have to recruit and train the interviewers. This will apply whether the interviewers are to be paid or are unpaid volunteers (see Chapter 3). Before you begin the process of recruitment, you will need to decide how many interviewers you need. This will vary depending on the size of the community you are profiling and the length of time you have available to do the work. In general, it is probably better to have as few interviewers as possible unless you are using local volunteers and the profiling exercise is being used to develop local people's skills, confidence and awareness (see Chapter 3). From a practical point of view, it is easier to manage the process and ensure consistency if relatively few people are involved. If you have sufficient people within the group involved in the profiling exercise with the necessary time and skills, then you will be able to avoid the lengthy task of recruitment described below. However, you should be careful that the interviewers, if they are drawn from the project group, are not seen by the community as an exclusive clique.

Recruitment

Whether your interviewers are going to be paid or not, you will probably want to recruit people who are part of the community to be profiled or have some knowledge of it. This means that you can probably restrict advertisements to the locality in the case of a geographically located community or to places or papers that are targeted at a particular group in the case of a community of interest. Any advertisement, whether it is a notice in a community centre or in the 'situations vacant' column of your local newspaper, needs to give the title of the project, what is entailed in the job (e.g. interviewing people in their own homes), how many hours, days and weeks of work are required, what skills or expertise you are looking for (e.g. sensitivity, knowledge of an ethnic minority language) and, if appropriate, what the rate of pay will be. Don't forget to include a contact point for further information, details of how people should go about applying for the jobs and the deadline for applications.

One way of recruiting interviewers is to advertise an open recruitment session at an appropriate venue or venues and invite interested people to come and talk about the project at a particular time. If you are going to use this method, you will need to make sure that you have enough people from the steering group or management group available to assist with interviewing and that you are there throughout the day and evening so that people in different circumstances can attend. It is a good idea to ask people to complete a simple application form in order to get basic information, such as name, address, telephone number, any relevant experience, availability for work and so on. You should also ask for the names and addresses of two referees. If you are sending people out to talk to people in their own homes, then it is only fair that you have taken some steps to establish that they are of good character.

Once applicants have completed their application form, you could then interview them to assess their suitability. This is best done with two people interviewing each candidate. If you are expecting a lot of candidates you may want to devise a simple form that can be used by the interviewers to record their impressions of the candidates and their suitability for the work. It goes without saying that the basic principles of equal opportunities procedures should apply, namely that you should only take into account relevant characteristics, qualifications and experience.

Once you have selected your interviewers, you should write to them to confirm that they have been appointed setting out the terms of the job. Your letter should make it clear that they are required to attend a training session on a particular day and that they should bring with them a passport-sized photograph to that session to be used for their identification card.

Training

The training of interviewers, whether paid or unpaid, is vital if the survey is to be successful. You will need a room large enough to accommodate comfortably the group of interviewers and trainers and to devise a programme for the training day or days. Figure 6.4 provides a checklist of issues that should be covered. These will be discussed briefly in turn. Most of what follows relates particularly to surveys involving face-to-face structured interviews with people in their own homes. However, some will also be of relevance to

Figure 6.4 Checklist of issues to be covered in interviewer training

- What is the survey about?
- Who is organizing the survey?
- Familiarization with survey materials
- Setting up interviews
- Working with quotas
- Introductions
- Interviewing techniques
- Confidentiality
- Recording responses
- Personal security
- Dealing with difficult situations
- Survey administration
- Finishing the interview
- Quality controls and back-checking

other kinds of interview surveys. At the end of this section, we include some issues of particular relevance to street interviewing, telephone interviewing, semi-structured interviews and group discussions.

What is the survey about?
It is important that the interviewers understand why the survey is taking place, what kinds of information is to be collected and why and what will happen to the information once it has been collated and analysed. The better their understanding of the survey, the more committed they are likely to be and the better will be the quality of the information that they collect; if the interviewers know what you are interested in, they are more likely to be able to record this information accurately. Also, it is important that the interviewers can confidently answer the questions of those who they are seeking to interview about the nature and purpose of the survey.

Who is organizing the survey?
Interviewers need to know exactly who is organizing the survey and to be able to answer questions about this from potential interviewees who may be highly suspicious of someone appearing on their doorstep armed with a clipboard.

Familiarization with survey materials
The more familiar interviewers are with the survey questionnaire
or interview schedule, the more confident they will be in the interview and the more accurate will be the information that you will
obtain. It is a good idea to go through the questionnaire explaining
what information each question is seeking, how any filter questions
work, giving examples of responses and inviting questions. Once
you have done this, you should allow as much time as possible for
the interviewers to practise using the questionnaire with each other.
One way of doing this is to work through the questionnaire with
all the interviewers in a group taking it in turns to ask each consecutive question. You may then want to allow time for them to
work in pairs taking it in turns to role-play interviewees.

Setting up interviews
The interviewers will need to understand fully how they are to find
people to interview. This will depend on the kind of sample you
are using. In most cases, the interviewers will be given a list of addresses to call on, or named individuals within identifiable
households or the names of streets with an instruction to call at
every 'nth' house. Whichever method you use, make sure that the
interviewers have appropriate written instructions which they can
refer back to. The interviewers also need instructions on when to
call on potential interviewees and how often they should call back
if they are not at home. A common method of working is to suggest
that people do not begin interviewing before ten o'clock in the
morning and should not work past nine o'clock at night and that
you should allow up to three visits on different days and at different
times of the day to try to catch people at home. Any calls to a particular address should be recorded either on the front of the interview schedule or on a separate record sheet.

Working with quotas
If you are using a system of quotas, the interviewers will need
details of how the quota system works and how to keep records
(see section on Quota Sampling above).

Introductions
How interviewers introduce themselves to potential interviewees is
likely to influence whether or not the interviewee agrees to be interviewed. It is a good idea to get each interviewer to come up with
a form of words which they feel comfortable with. This should

Figure 6.5 Interviewer introductions: A checklist of tips

- Say who you are and what organization you are from
- Show your identification card and invite the interviewee to check it
- Tell the interviewee about the survey. It might be helpful to show them a copy of a publicity leaflet if one has been produced to jog their memory
- Check who you are speaking to and invite them to be interviewed if they are the right person or ask to speak to someone else in the household if not
- Be prepared to answer any questions that might be asked: How long will it take? How did you get hold of my name? What will happen to the information?
- Give an assurance of confidentiality
- If the person appears reluctant to be interviewed, try to find out why they are unwilling and give answers to their objections. But accept that they have the right to refuse to participate
- Be friendly, confident and enthusiastic about the survey.

explain who they are, who they are working for and the fact that they would like to interview the person concerned. Where a named individual is being sought within the household or a quota sample is being used, then they also need to find appropriate words to check that they are talking to the right person. Figure 6.5 provides a checklist of issues relevant to introductions.

Interviewing techniques
The interviewers will need some basic training in interviewing techniques. Much of this is common sense and will come naturally to anyone with good listening skills. However, there are some issues which ought to be emphasized. These include the importance of reading the question exactly as it appears in the questionnaire, not prompting the respondent except where there is a specific instruction to 'probe', showing that they are listening to the respondent by nodding and smiling, remaining neutral with regards the content of the questions and the answers – neither agreeing or disagreeing – and not getting drawn in to arguments or discussions with the interviewee.

Confidentiality
The importance of confidentiality should be stressed throughout

the training. The interviewers must understand the importance of not discussing the content of interviews with others and of keeping all completed interview schedules in a secure place. Arrangements should be made for the interviewers to return completed questionnaires to the survey organizers as soon as possible after completion.

Recording responses
The interviewers should practise recording responses to questions during their training. They need to understand the importance of working through the questionnaire systematically, carefully following any instructions. All responses should be recorded accurately and honestly. If the interviewer is unsure of how to record a response or which category to put it in, they should be instructed to make a note on the form detailing the precise answer and to then check with the survey organizer precisely how the answer should be recorded. The general rule should be that if they are in any doubt, they should write down more rather than less information. This is especially the case with open-ended questions. For precoded questions, the appropriate box should be ticked or the appropriate response circled clearly. If an interviewer makes a mistake or a respondent changes his or her mind, then make sure that the intended response is clearly identified.

If the respondent answers 'none' to a question, then this should be written on the form. Leaving a blank or putting a dash might be interpreted as the question was refused or not asked. All responses should be written clearly, especially when someone else has responsibility for coding, inputting and analysing the information.

After the interview has been completed, the interviewer should check through the form to make sure that all responses are legible and that no questions have been missed. It is a good idea for the interviewers to be encouraged to make comments about the process, e.g. difficulties with the interview itself, problems in using the questionnaire and so on.

Personal security
All interviewers should be fully briefed on personal security. This briefing should stress the importance of carrying their identification card with them at all times. This card should have a picture of the interviewer, his or her name, the name of the organization carrying out the survey and it should be signed by a representative of that organization. It should also have a telephone number which

interviewees can ring in order to verify the identity of the interviewer. The interviewers should also have written down an emergency telephone number which they can ring if they have a problem. It is a good idea to inform the local police station in writing that a survey is being conducted in a particular area, giving them the dates, the names of the interviewers and their car registrations where appropriate. It is usually best to send interviewers out to work particular streets or areas in pairs with an instruction that they contact the survey organizers if one of them has not seen the other for a while. Depending on the areas in which they are working, it can sometimes be helpful to equip interviewers with personal alarms and dog dazers.

In general, personal security relies on the good sense of the interviewers, although the above precautions will help protect them while they are out in the field. The basic rule should be that interviewers should take appropriate steps to minimize risk and should back off from any situation in which they feel uncomfortable, even if this means terminating an interview prematurely. One way of doing this is for interviewers to look at their watch and say they have to check back with a colleague.

Survey organizers not only have a duty to take appropriate steps to protect their interviewers, they also have a duty to protect those who they are interviewing. This means that interviewers should be trustworthy and be provided with character references from appropriate referees. You may also want to think carefully about what kind of interviewer you employ for particular projects.

Dealing with difficult situations
The interviewers need to be given advice during their training about dealing with difficult or potentially difficult situations. Interviewing people about issues that are important to them can arouse strong feelings of anger or distress. The interviewers need to have some idea of what to do in these situations. Again common sense and sensitivity will cover most situations. However, it is a good idea to remind the interviewers that it is not their job to engage with the emotions of those who they are interviewing or to offer counselling or advice. If an interviewee is clearly upset or angered by a particular question, the interviewer might gently suggest that they move on to the next one or suggest that they terminate the interview. The interviewers should never promise interviewees that they will take action on their behalf.

Finishing the interview
When the interviewer has worked through the questionnaire, the interviewee should be given the opportunity to make any general comments about the content of the survey and on the way it has been carried out. It is also a good idea to leave them with a leaflet which thanks them for taking part and informs them what will happen next.

Survey administration
The interviewers need to be provided with the basic tools which are required to undertake the interviews (see Fig. 6.6). They also need to know where to come to get new interview schedules and further names and addresses and where and how often they should return completed questionnaires. If the interviewers are to be paid, you will also need to deal with issues relating to pay, expenses and national insurance.

Quality controls and back-checking
All completed questionnaires need to be checked for accuracy and to make sure that they contain no ambiguities (see also section on Coding and Editing in Chapter 7). You may also want to do back-checking. This means that the survey organizer contacts a sample of those interviewed to check that the interviewer did call on them at the time stated on the form, that the interview was conducted in a satisfactory manner and that certain basic items of information (especially those pertaining to quotas) have been recorded accurately.

Figure 6.6 Interviewers' materials

- Pens and pencils
- Clipboard
- Blank questionnaires
- Paper
- Map of the area
- Contact names of key local people
- Emergency phone numbers
- Identification card
- Quota instructions
- List of names and/or addresses
- Publicity leaflets about the survey
- Thank you leaflets

Street interviews

If your survey is to be based on face-to-face interviews in the street or other public place, there are two main implications for survey design and interviewer training. The first is for the length of the questionnaire. People interviewed in the street are less likely to be willing to spend more than a few minutes talking to you. As a result, your questionnaire will have to be quite short and include many easily answered tick box questions. Second, you cannot know in advance who will be in your sample. As a result, you will almost certainly have to construct quotas and train interviewers in how to select likely looking people. While this is usually easy with regard to characteristics like gender, it is much more difficult to assess someone's age, let alone their employment status simply by looking at them. Interviewers may have to approach people and ask them whether they conform to the quota characteristics they are looking for using a standard screening question before embarking on the interview. This can be difficult, since people may be sensitive about being asked their age, ethnic background or employment status. The training of interviewers who are going to be doing street interviewing must address these issues.

Telephone interviewing

There are three main implications for survey design and interviewer training of doing a telephone survey. The first relates to the type of questionnaire to be used. It would be inappropriate, in most cases, to use a telephone survey for in-depth, qualitative interviewing. Lack of face-to-face, personal contact means that it is very difficult to build up the requisite rapport and trust between interviewer and interviewee that is necessary for this kind of survey. Telephone surveys work best with questionnaires that are short, to the point and consist mainly of tick-box questions. The second implication is that interviewers must take steps to establish that they are speaking to an appropriate person. Again, if they are working to quotas, this might be by asking a set of screening questions or, if they have a sample of named individuals, by checking that they have the right person. The third issue relates to persuading people to be interviewed. It is generally much easier for someone to refuse an unseen 'voice' at the end of a 'phone than a 'real' person on the doorstep. Interviewer training for telephone surveys should look in particular at techniques of persuading people not only to participate but not to hang up.

Semi-structured interviews

Much of what we have said about undertaking interview surveys will also apply to conducting semi-structured interviews. However, there are a number of issues that are especially relevant to this kind of method. First, semi-structured interviews can be quite lengthy, so it is important that the interviewee knows this in advance and has the necessary time available. For this reason, it is often wise to contact the interviewees in advance to arrange appropriately timed appointments. Second, semi-structured interviews, because they are much more like a dialogue, entail the interviewer being confident and knowledgeable about the issues under discussion so that they are able to ask appropriate supplementary questions. This is especially important when interviewing professional people or service providers. Third, by their nature, semi-structured interviews are not amenable to recording responses through ticking boxes. It may therefore be necessary for interviewers to tape-record interviews as well as making some notes during the interview. The interview should then be written up as soon as possible following completion using both notes and tape-recording to remind the interviewer of what was said. However, the interviewers must get the agreement of the interviewees to tape the interview.

Group discussions

Undertaking group discussions entails very different techniques and skills to individual interviewing. First, an appropriate group has to be assembled. You may want to invite community or voluntary groups to send a certain number of representatives or you might want to organize a discussion with a group of people drawn from a particular street or who are involved in the provision of a certain service to the community. In general, the group should consist of no more than seven or eight people with two facilitators to guide and record the discussion.

The group should meet in an informal setting such as someone's living room and should be scheduled to last for about one and a half hours. The role of the facilitator is to introduce the themes for discussion, encourage as many people as possible to participate and

ensure that no-one in the group dominates the discussion or inti-
midates others. This requires particular skills and it may be a good
idea to try to find someone to fulfil this role who has had experience of doing group work. The other facilitator needs to keep a
record of the meeting, including: date and venue of meeting; details
of who participated; and points raised in discussion. As with semi-
structured interviews, a tape-recorder can be useful provided the
group members agree to its use. Detailed notes of the meeting,
including the facilitator's observations, should be written up as
soon as possible after the meeting.

Managing interview surveys

All surveys require someone or a small group to act as survey coor-
dinators. This is especially important with interview surveys, since
the coordinator will have responsibility not only for managing a
process – ensuring that things get sent to the right people at the
right time – but also a group of people. Whether they are paid or
not, the survey coordinator will have the major responsibility
for ensuring that the interviewers carry out the survey to an acceptable standard and in an appropriate manner, that they have the
materials that they require, that they are not put at risk and that
they receive appropriate support and management.

Key issues

This rather lengthy and, at times, technical chapter has taken the
reader through some basic techniques of survey methodology. If the
instructions are followed carefully, it should enable you to undertake an interview or self-completion survey that will result in good-
quality, reliable and accurate information. However, undertaking
a survey can be a lengthy and resource-intensive task and should
not be embarked upon lightly.

Further reading

Bell, J. (1993) *Doing Your Research Project*, 2nd edn. Buckingham: Open
    University Press.
Kane, E. (1991) *Doing Your Own Research*. London: Marion Boyars.

Kingsley, S. and Taylor, M. (1985) *Research in Voluntary and Community Organisations: Some Guidelines for Employing Researchers.* Wivenhoe: ARVAC.

Nachmias, C. and Nachmias, D. (1989) *Research Methods in the Social Sciences.* London: Edward Arnold.

de Vaus, D.A. (1991) *Surveys in Social Research.* London: Allen and Unwin.

7

Storing and analysing information

Introduction

Once you have undertaken a survey to collect primary data, you will then need to make sense of the data set and use it to construct your profile. Moving from a pile of questionnaires to useful and relevant information requires a number of different processes. These include preparing, storing, analysing and presenting the data in an appropriate form (see Fig. 7.1). These processes are necessary whether you intend to sort, store and analyse your data manually or use a computer, and whether your data are predominantly quantitative or qualitative.

In this chapter, we begin by looking at manual and computer analysis and the issues relevant to deciding between the two. We then take you through the various processes involved in preparing, storing, analysing and presenting quantitative data. We will then look at the use of computers in handling survey data and techniques involved in the analysis of qualitative data. As was the case with the previous chapter, this chapter will provide you with the basic information you need to be able to use the data obtained from a community-profiling exercise without providing in-depth knowledge of statistical techniques as such.

Options for storing and analysing data

There are essentially two options for storing and analysing data – manually or by computer. In deciding which method to use, you will need to take account of the following considerations: the size of the survey, the type of questions asked and the type of analysis required; the equipment you have available; and the skills that exist within your project group. These issues should have been

Figure 7.1   From data to information: Processes

Manual analysis	Computer analysis
• Edit and code the data	• Edit and code the data
• Set up a data summary sheet	• Set up a data entry form
• Summarize the data from the questionnaires onto summary sheets	• Input the data from the questionnaires
	• Import the data into an analysis package
• Check the data	• Check and clean the data
• Undertake analysis required	• Undertake analysis required
• Produce output in the form of tables, graphs, etc.	• Produce output in the form of tables, graphs, etc.

considered at the beginning of the project, and certainly at the time that the questionnaire was designed (see Chapter 6). Failure to make decisions at the planning stage can result in problems later. For example, if you have used a long questionnaire with a very large sample, it will be virtually impossible to analyse the information without a computer. If you did not take account of this before you started, you may well end up with a large pile of questionnaires which you cannot effectively analyse.

Manual analysis requires little more than person power, time, pens, paper and a calculator. Computer analysis requires a computer, appropriate software and people with the skills to use it. In general, manual analysis is only appropriate where the survey is quite small and for qualitative data (see later section). Although we take you through the processes involved in the manual analysis of data, we would recommend that you try to get access to a computer if at all possible.

Preparing data

Whether you intend to analyse your data manually or use a computer, it will first be necessary to edit and code completed questionnaires. What follows relates primarily to questionnaires which contain predominantly quantitative data. The relevant processes that need to be gone through to analyse qualitative data are described in a later section.

The process of editing and coding will make summarizing the data for manual analysis or entering the data into a computer quicker and reduce the chances of error. The process of editing requires checking through all returned questionnaires to ensure there are no obvious mistakes and that the right questions have been answered. This is especially important if you used a self-completion questionnaire or where the questionnaire involved a large number of filter questions, both of which increase the chances of questions being missed, misinterpreted or incorrectly completed. Any such questions should be clearly identified so that only correct and appropriate information is included.

At the completion of the editing process, the response to each question should be clear, a consistent approach to different types of responses should have been agreed upon and there should be no omissions. At this point, coding can begin. It is possible to combine the editing and coding processes. However, this may have the effect of reducing the speed of coding.

Coding refers to the assignment of numerical codes to non-numerical responses so that statistical analysis can take place. In order to do this, you will require a coding frame, which essentially lists the possible responses to each question and the numerical value that corresponds to them. One way of drawing up a coding frame is to take a 10 per cent sample of returned questionnaires and check the range of responses for each question. These can then be listed or grouped as appropriate and numerical values assigned. Where the survey questionnaire has used a large number of closed questions, then this is a simple task as the responses are largely given. However, where an open question is asked such as, What additional services or facilities would you like to see provided in your community?, the list of responses must be derived from the sample of completed questionnaires and the appropriate code assigned to it. Using the coding frame as a guide, the person coding the questionnaire will then need to go through all questionnaires writing the code number for the response next to it.

Storing the data

Once edited and coded, the data set will have to be stored in such a way that it can than be analysed. It is possible to do this manually or by using a computer. If you are intending to analyse the data manually, you will need to record the responses to all questions in such a way that you can make sense of the data set and get it to answer certain questions. This will involve reading through all the questionnaires and recording all the responses on summary sheets. Where the question is closed it will involve totalling the answers, and where the questions are open it will involve writing down the answers on a summary sheet. Figure 7.2 gives examples of some survey questions with the codes identified. Figure 7.3 shows how this information could be recorded manually using a summary sheet.[1]

In the example summary sheet in Fig. 7.3, each respondent has been given a unique number which should be written on the questionnaire and can serve two purposes. First, it allows responses to be matched to questionnaires. This may be important if any inconsistencies are discovered in the data. It can also be used for analysis purposes. In the example, we have created a respondent number with three parts: the first is a continuous number to distinguish between respondents; the second records the sex of the respondent; and the third is a code for age. Using the information from the summary sheets, it is a relatively easy task to work out how many men and women, respectively, say they are satisfied with a particular service or whether people in any one age group are more likely than others to express satisfaction or dissatisfaction.

Figure 7.2   Examples of survey questions

1. Would you like to see more services provided in your area? (CIRCLE ONE)
   Yes 1
   No 2
2. If you have used any of the following services, please say how satisfied you are with them? (CIRCLE ONE RESPONSE FOR EACH LINE)

	very satisfied	satisfied	dissatisfied	very dissatisfied	don't know
Home help	1	2	3	4	5
Social worker	1	2	3	4	5
Day centre	1	2	3	4	5

3. How many years have you lived at your current address? (CIRCLE ONE)
   0–10 11–20 21–30 31–40 41–50 51–60 61–70 71–80
4. How old were you at your last birthday? (PLEASE WRITE IN)
5. What additional services or facilities would you like to see in your community? (PLEASE WRITE IN)

Figure 7.3 Manual summary sheet

Respondent	Question 1 1 2	Question 2 1 2 3 4 5	Question 3 1 2 3 4 5 6 7 8	
01/M/3	1	1	1	
02/F/4	1	1	1	

Responses to open questions which cannot be assigned a numerical code may be more difficult to summarize in this way. Where the responses to open questions are lengthy and quite varied, then the best method is to write the responses in full on pieces of paper grouped according to characteristics such as the gender, age and employment status of the respondent.

If you are intending to use a computer to undertake the analysis, then you have a number of choices regarding storage of data. You can either use an integrated package which has its own data entry module (see section on Using computers for storing and analysing data, below) or, alternatively, you can enter the responses into the computer using a data entry package of which there are a number. These are software packages designed for the input of numerical data. Another method is to enter the data into a database or spreadsheet package.

Once you have entered the data into the package, it is a good idea to run a set of frequencies to check that it makes sense. Should there be any values or variables that should not be there, you will want to check the original questionnaire and then go into the data entry package and amend the data. It is probably a good idea to check a sample of cases against the original questionnaire to ensure they have been input accurately. If the number of responses is not too large, then the sample should be about 10 per cent.

Analysing the data

Once stored in coded format either on a summary sheet or in a computer file, the data can be analysed. Essentially, what is meant by data analysis is getting the data to answer certain questions. Quantitative data enable you to ask questions which take the form how many or what proportion? In addition, you can ask questions about the relationships between variables or items of information. In deciding what kinds of analysis you want to do, you will need to consider two main issues: What questions are you trying to answer? And how many variables will you want to look at simultaneously?

Questions to ask

In any community profile, there are certain questions which you will almost certainly want to ask your data. The most basic information that you will require is the number and percentage of people who responded in particular ways to each question that was asked in the survey. These are called frequencies (see below). You will almost certainly want to ask questions about the responses of particular groups of people categorized by, for example, age, gender, ethnicity, employment status and so on. Beyond this basic information, you will need to think what other issues you want to address in your analysis. For example, you might want to test a hypothesis about a particular phenomenon by looking at the data set to see if it supports your hypothesis. Again your ability to do this is greatly enhanced if you have access to a computer and appropriate software (see below).

How many variables?

One of the main issues you will have to address is how many variables you want to include in your analysis. To count the number of respondents who are male and female and to present that information as a numerical value or as a percentage is termed univariate analysis. However, you may also want to look at the relationship between two variables, for example gender and qualifications. This is called bivariate analysis and would enable you to say, for example, that 33 per cent of women respondents have no formal qualifications. However, you may also want to look at the relationship between more than two variables, that is, multivariate analysis. This would enable you to make statements like: 90 per cent of women with no qualifications have an annual income of less than £5000. The more variables involved, the more complex the analysis. It is therefore important to decide what level of analysis is appropriate to the aims, objectives and overall purpose of your profile.

Basic statistics[2]

Any community profile will contain some statistics. Statistics are essentially a numerical way of representing information. There are three main kinds of statistics that you will need to know about: frequencies, averages and cross-tabulations.

Frequencies

Frequencies describe the number of times a particular value occurs in the data set. Frequencies may be expressed as whole numbers or percentages. So, for example, gender is a variable with two values, that is, male and female. If your data set contains responses from 200 people of whom 120 (or 60 per cent) are women and 80 (or 40 per cent) are men, then this is the frequency for the variable 'gender'.

Averages

There are three ways of expressing an average: mode, median or mean. Which one you use will depend on the type of variable and the way in which the information was stored. For example, if we take a variable like age of respondents, the frequency distribution might be as shown in Fig. 7.4. To work out the average age of respondents, it is necessary to add together the ages of all respondents (2017) and divide by the number of respondents (50) to give a mean age of 40.3 years.

Figure 7.4   Age distribution (notional)

Age of respondents (years)	Number	Percentage
21	3	6
25	7	2
29	6	12
34	10	20
38	5	10
42	6	12
47	2	4
54	3	6
63	1	2
68	3	6
75	4	8
Total	50	100

Figure 7.5 Length of time at current address (notional)

Years	Number	Percentage	Cumulative percentage
<1	13	26	26
1–5	15	30	56
6–10	8	16	72
11–15	6	12	84
15–20	3	6	90
> 20	5	10	100

If, however, the ages of respondents were stored in bands (e.g. 20–29, 30–39, 40–49, 50–59, 60–69 and 70 and over), it would not be possible to compute the mean age. In this case, it would be better to use either the median or mode. The median is the middle place on a ranking scale. In the example shown in Fig. 7.5, the median length of time that respondents have lived at their current address is 1–5 years, as this is the category which includes the 50 per cent mark. In this example, the median is also the mode. The mode is the single most common response. In this case, 30 out of 50 lived at their current address for 1–5 years, which is the single largest response category.

Cross-tabulation

So far we have looked only at a single variable. However, you will almost certainly want to look at the relationship between two or more variables. For example, we might want to look at the relationship between gender and the wish to see more services provided in the area (see Fig. 7.6).

This is a cross-tabulation of two variables and it indicates that there may be a relationship between the gender of respondents and their response to this particular question, which allows us to say that women are more likely to express a desire for additional

Figure 7.6 Gender × wish to see additional services (notional)

	More services (%)	No more services (%)
Men	33.3	66.6
Women	76.9	23.1

services. This is important for two reasons. First, it might suggest further lines of enquiry such as finding out (perhaps using one of the other methods suggested in Chapter 5) exactly what services women feel are lacking or to interrogate the data set further to see if it can tell us anything else about this issue, for example the age of women seeking additional services, whether or not they have children and whether or not they are in employment. This might involve looking at three variables simultaneously, for example gender, desire for additional services and employment status. It can be very time-consuming and difficult to try to do this kind of analysis without a computer. The more complex the analysis you undertake, the more difficult it may be to draw conclusions about which you are confident, since the cell size – in other words, the number of responses in each box of your table – may be too small.

Presenting quantitative information

Statistical data can often be very difficult to interpret, absorb and understand. However, there are a number of different ways in which statistical information can be presented that makes data easier to understand. 'The most important rule in communicating quantitative information is to THINK CLEARLY. If you know exactly what your data say you will have little difficulty in communicating the message effectively'.[3] In other words, in order to convey statistical information to others, you must understand what it means yourself and also know what is important and what is not. There are three main ways of presenting quantitative information: tables, graphs or charts, and words. Which of these you use will depend on the type of information that you are wanting to put across. Chapman notes that 'tables are best for conveying numerical values, pictures are best for conveying qualitative relationships and words are best for conveying implications for action'.[4]

Tables

A table is essentially a way of summarizing numerical or statistical information. Many people are put off reading a report if it contains too many tables. Any table that you use should be necessary, clear and be referred to in the text. Figure 7.7 makes some general points about tables.

Figure 7.7 General points about tables

Every table should:
- contain enough information so that it can be read on its own
- have a consecutive number and an appropriate title
- use a standard format
- be discussed in the text to reinforce the message
- be carefully selected (Is it really necessary?)
- have rounded figures to demonstrate a point
- have figures in columns to aid comprehension and mental arithmetic
- order categories by size so that the largest is first
- use footnotes to explain or qualify any figures or sections
- provide a reference to its source if it is not primary data
- have figures being compared in columns
- break long columns up – groups of 5 is suggested

Charts

Charts are graphical ways of demonstrating the relationship between variables. The three types of chart that you are most likely to find useful are pie charts, line graphs and bar charts. Figure 7.8 makes some general points of relevance to all three kinds of charts.

Pie charts are particularly useful in demonstrating the relative proportions of sub-groups making up a whole. For example, Fig. 7.9 is a pie chart which shows the proportions of a survey response sample who have been resident at their current address for different lengths of time. *Line graphs* are useful for highlighting changes over time. For example, Fig. 7.10 shows the monthly figures for reported crimes over a year. From this graph, it is very

Figure 7.8 General points about charts

Charts should:
- be numbered and have an appropriate title
- be discussed in the text
- show units and scales of measurement
- not include too much information
- have 'graphical integrity', i.e. they represent what they are supposed to represent
- be easy to read and interpret

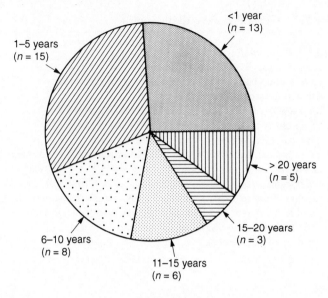

Numbers of respondents

Figure 7.9 Example pie chart: Length of time at current address

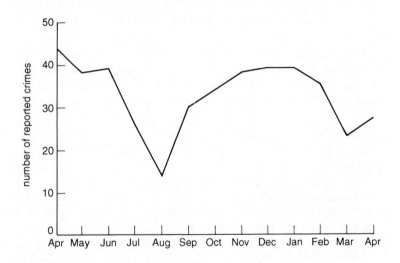

Figure 7.10 Example line of graph: Number of reported crimes

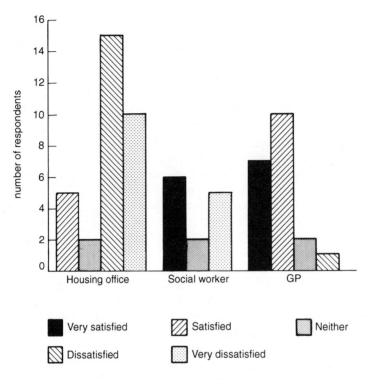

Figure 7.11   Example bar chart: Satisfaction with services

easy to see that the crime figures dipped sharply in July and August to rise again in September. *Bar charts* can be used to show the relative size of groups and changes over time and, in addition, can be used to illustrate the relationship between two or more variables. For example, Fig. 7.11 is a bar chart showing the number of respondents expressing satisfaction with a number of different services. From this chart, it is easy to see that the housing office attracted more dissatisfied responses than did social workers or GPs.

A community profile can be considerably enhanced by appropriate use of tables, graphs and charts. However, they will still require comment in the written part of the report. You will need to refer to them and draw the reader's attention to the key point that they are being used to demonstrate and also draw out the implications from them.

Using computers for storing and analysing data

The use of computers in survey research and statistical analysis is now extremely common and many books on survey research do not even consider manual analysis of the survey data. There are now many packages on the market which can be used in survey research and which vary in price and sophistication. Whichever software package or packages are used, the procedures for storing and analysing the data will be similar.

There are software packages for inputting data, analysing data and producing graphical output, and some integrated packages that perform all the functions required for survey analysis. Before choosing a package, one will need to consider the issues indicated in Fig. 7.12. If you have little or no knowledge of computer packages, then ease of use, a telephone helpline, menu system and good documentation will be especially important in selecting the appropriate software package.

There are several integrated packages that you might want to consider. These vary in price and sophistication. If your study is being undertaken in a rural area, you might want to consider an integrated package called 'Village Appraisal'. This software package is designed specifically for community profiles of small villages or rural areas (see Fig. 7.13).[5]

SNAP is another integrated package for survey analysis, although considerably more expensive (in 1992, SNAP II was £695). Like Village Appraisal, it employs a menu system and is easy to use for the simple analysis of survey data. The data can be entered, stored, analysed and tables generated. Frequencies and

Figure 7.12 Issues to consider when selecting a software package

- Will the software run on your computer?
- Will the software perform all the tasks that you require, e.g. data entry, analysis, etc.?
- Will it produce the kinds of statistics that you require?
- Can the software package cope with the size of your data set?
- How much can you afford to spend?
- Is there a telephone help line?
- Is the software user-friendly?
- Does the package include training?
- Are the manuals easy to use?

Figure 7.13   Village Appraisal integrated software package[6]

Village Appraisal is an integrated software package which contains
three 'units':
• CREATE creates a questionnaire from a database of 400 questions
  from which the user can select up to 80 questions. In addition,
  a limited number of questions specific to the community under
  study can be included. The questionnaire is then printed out.
• DATAIN allows the user to enter the responses to the questions.
• ANALYZE undertakes the analysis and prints the results in either
  graphical or tabular form. The analysis consists of frequencies for
  each question and some multivariate analysis is also possible. A
  basic report is produced which can be imported into a word-
  processing package.
This package has the advantage of being cheap, it costs £50, and
it can save a great deal of time as it is integrated and easy to use.
The main drawback is that it is limited in terms of the analysis that
can be performed. However, in most cases, it will probably be
sufficient.

cross-tabulations can be easily produced. However, like Village
Appraisal, it cannot undertake any sophisticated statistical analysis. In an evaluation of software for statistical analysis, the conclusion on SNAP was: 'It does the basic tasks well and simply'.[7]

Possibly the most commonly used software package for survey
research is Statistical Package for the Social Sciences (SPSS). SPSS
has a number of modules. For three modules to enter data, analyse
data and produce tables, the price is similar to that for SNAP. The
data entry module and base modules would be sufficient to enter
and store data and then analyse the data. However, additional
modules are required for quality graphical and tabular output.
SPSS is not as easy to use as Village Appraisal or SNAP, and despite
menu options it can often be user-unfriendly. However, having
learned how to use it, SPSS is extremely powerful and can undertake as much statistical analysis as one could ever require from
survey data.

There are a number of other packages such as Quantime,[8]
which was developed for the market research industry. This has
modules which can undertake questionnaire design and production, computer-assisted telephone interviewing (CATI), computer-
assisted personal interviewing (CAPI), Data Entry, Desktop

tabulation, editing and tabulation of data. It goes without saying that this package is not cheap.

It is possible to use database or spreadsheet packages for certain stages of the research process. They tend to be limited in terms of data analysis but can be useful for data entry. Once the data set has been entered, it can then be imported into another package for statistical analysis such as SPSS, Statgraphics or Minitab.

Analysing qualitative data

If the research involves in-depth interviews, focus groups or public meetings, then the type of analysis required will be different to that for a self-completion questionnaire or a structured interview. As with quantitative analysis, one can analyse qualitative data either manually or using a computer package. Computer packages for analysing qualitative information are less common than those for use in analysing quantitative data, but the selection is growing. As a general rule, if the survey involves long, semi-structured interviews with a large sample, then using a computer package will aid the analysis and make it more efficient.

How should one begin to analyse a pile of questionnaires without using a computer? There are two initial tasks: first, each questionnaire must be assigned a unique number and, second, each questionnaire must be photocopied. Having read through the questionnaires, they then need to be 'deconstructed'. This involves the careful use of a pair of scissors to cut up the written information according to the main themes or issues. A number of different coloured highlighting pens are useful for marking key issues and telling quotes. Each piece of paper should have the respondent's identification number written on it so that the source of the information can be traced back to the original. It is also useful to make a note of the respondent's characteristics (age, gender, ethnicity, etc.). Once the data have been sorted in this way, you should be able to read through all the material noting the key issues.

Computer packages for the analysis of qualitative data work in essentially the same way. The first task is to type all the text into a word-processing package. Once the text has been checked, it should be saved as an ASCII file ready for import into a qualitative analysis package. Having transferred the text into the software package, you will then need to print it out and decide which sections are important. These sections then have to be coded. Once this process is complete, the data can be analysed. If you intend to use a qualitative package to analyse the data, you should be prepared to invest considerable resources in terms of both time and money. However, a project that contained a large qualitative element would be difficult to undertake using manual methods of analysis.

Key issues

Analysing data is often easier to do than read about. Most community profiles can be produced using only frequencies and some cross-tabulations, with perhaps some verbatim comments drawn from interviews or group discussions. If an integrated package such as SNAP or Village Appraisal is used, then this process can be quite straightforward. In deciding whether to analyse data manually or by using a computer, and in considering which software package to use, you will need to consider how large your survey is, what analysis is required, what expertise is available and what resources are available.

Further reading

Bell, J. (1993) *Doing Your Research Project*: 2nd edn, Ch. 11. Buckingham: Open University Press.

Fielding, N.G. and Lee, R.M. (eds) (1991) *Using Computers in Qualitative Research*. London: Sage.

Fowler, F.J. (1988) *Survey Research Methods*, Ch. 8. London: Sage.

Rowntree, D. (1981) *Statistics Without Tears: A Primer for Non-mathematicians*. Harmondsworth: Pelican.

Tesch, R. (1990) *Qualitative Research: Analysis Types and Software Tools*. Lewes: Falmer Press.

de Vaus, D.A. (1990) *Surveys in Social Research*, 2nd edn, Parts III and IV. London: Unwin-Hyman.

Westlake, A. *et al.* (eds) (1992) *Survey and Statistical Computing: Proceedings of an International Conference Organised by the Study Group on Computers in Survey Analysis*. Amsterdam: Elsvier.

Notes

1. See also Bell, J. (1993) *Doing Your Research Project*, pp. 106–108. Buckingham: Open University Press; Hoinville, G. *et al.* (1977) *Survey Research Practice*, p. 173. London: Gower.

2. This section on basic statistics will be covered by most books on statistics. If you have basic statistical knowledge, then this section can be omitted from your reading.
3. Chapman, M. (1986) *Plain Figures*, p. 20. London: HMSO.
4. Ibid., p. 11.
5. The Policy Research Unit at Leeds Metropolitan University is currently working with CCRU (who developed Village Appraisal) to develop an Urban Appraisal software package for use by people in an urban setting who wish to profile their community.
6. For more information on Village Appraisal, contact your local rural community council or The Countryside and Community Research Unit, Cheltenham and Gloucester College of Higher Education, Francis Close Hall, Swindon Road, Cheltenham GL50 4AZ (tel: 0242 532912).
7. Chell, M. (1992) 'A comparison of some software packages for survey analysis'. In Survey and Statistical Computing: *Proceedings of an International Conference Organised by the Study Group on Computers in Survey Analysis* (A. Westlake *et al.* eds). Amsterdam: Elsevier. op. cit. p. 394.
8. Quantime (n.d.) *The Quantime System: The Complete Data System for Market Research Surveys*. London: Quantime.

8
Collating and presenting information

Introduction

Once you have collected and analysed the information relevant to your community profile, you will need to bring it all together to form a coherent whole that effectively communicates your findings to the people you are trying to persuade, influence and inform. Although community profiles can take a variety of different forms (see Fig. 8.1), a written report is the most common way of presenting the finished profile, although you may also want to use other methods to highlight particular issues or to complement the written report (see also Chapter 9). The medium used to communicate your profile will be an important determinant of how effective it is.

This chapter takes you through the process of producing a community profile in the form of a written report. First, we look at some issues of relevance to communication and then look at the actual writing of the report before considering the options for production of the final document.

Figure 8.1 Options for presenting community-profiling information

- Written report
- Leaflet
- Summary report
- Video
- Presentation to public meeting
- Presentations to local groups
- Exhibition
- Local newsletter

What is communication?

Communication involves more than one person giving another person information. It involves one person sending a message and another receiving the message that the sender intended. Real communication can only be said to have taken place when the receiver understands the message that has been sent. In the case of a written report, there are two main reasons why effective communication may not take place. It could be that the report is not read because it is unattractive to the reader. For example, it may be too technical or too boring. Or it might be read but not understood. There are a number of ways of minimizing the chances of this happening to your profile and therefore maximizing its intended impact.

First, successful communication is likely to depend in part on the attitude of those communicating. Is there a *willingness to communicate* between those presenting the findings of the report and those receiving them? We have all seen politicians being interviewed on television wilfully ignoring the interviewer's questions, merely reiterating their own message. If one is trying to persuade a local authority that, for example, the community profiled lacks certain services, then it is important to write the report using arguments that have meaning for that organization. This might involve a reference to a declared commitment to equality of access or the provision of a basic standard of service. The tone of the report may also be important in this connection. A report that is aggressive in tone, while it may reflect the anger of the community profiled, may generate an equally aggressive response and therefore fail to achieve its purpose. A report that is well-structured, well-argued and supported by appropriate and accurate statistics is likely to be more persuasive in a majority of cases than a tub-thumping polemic.

Second, communication may fail if the author of the report, or the group under whose auspices the work was conducted, has no *credibility* with the intended audience. For example, a local group with a political bias may present a report to a local council of a different political complexion. The council may not accept the findings of a community-profiling exercise even where they are based on careful and appropriate research and analysis, because it suspects it of political bias. You should, of course, have addressed this issue at the beginning of your project when establishing the steering or management group. However, at the writing-up stage you may also want to consider whose name appears on the cover of the report.

Third, you should be clear about who the profile is aimed at and what is the general message that you are trying to convey. The way in which you answer these questions will affect the tone and style of your report. Fourth, you should ensure that the language used is appropriate to those people one is trying to communicate with. If your main audience is the local community, then the language used should be appropriate to that audience without talking down to them. If the main intended audience is an official body, then the style of the report may be different. You may find it helpful to look at an example of a report that has been produced for, say, a local authority committee to give you some idea of what is required. However, no matter who your intended audience, the language used should always be as simple and direct as possible.

The appearance of your report is another factor that is likely to influence whether or not it is an effective medium of communication. While graphic design has been around for quite a while, information design is a relatively new field. Information design has been described as being at the interface of information science and graphic design. Research reports are an area ripe for information design.[1] The Information Design Association defines information design as activities that contribute to the effective communication of information and as such it has relevance to the production of a community profile. The advent of desktop publishing software packages that can be run on most computer hardware means that many people can now produce professional looking documents quite cheaply. However, the person using such packages will still need some basic understanding of design principles to help him or her make decisions about lay-out, typeface, headings and sub-headings. It is also true that because well-produced publications can now be obtained relatively easily, expectations about the quality of publications in general have increased.

Writing the report

Ellis and Hopkins[2] note that there are four categories of report: informative, persuasive, explanatory and historical. A community profile is fairly unique in that it can be a combination of all these categories. It can inform local residents about the community they live in, persuade local policy makers of the need for action, explain the nature of local issues, and examine trends in the history of the community.

Any book on writing will emphasize the need to write for the intended audience and, as noted previously, communication will be more effective if language is appropriate, which implies that you know who you are writing for. What is the aim of the report? Your report will be seeking to persuade someone about something. You may wish to inform the council that facilities for local children are poor and persuade them to address this problem. You may be trying to evaluate the success of a local initiative for the local community. The aim may be to 'empower' the local community by providing the information to mobilize support for a campaign on a particular issue.

In addition to knowing the audience of the report, it is important that the steering group and authors of a report are explicit about the objectives of the report. There must be a definite purpose, so that the authors can think clearly and make the report intelligible to readers. If the authors are unclear in their thinking, then there will be little chance of communicating the contents of the report successfully to the reader.

One of the first issues to be decided upon is who is going to write the report. Will it be a team effort or the work of one individual? It may depend upon how the profile was carried out. If the bulk of work was undertaken by a single researcher, then it would make sense for that person to undertake the majority of the initial writing. If there is a committee managing the project, then it will save time and problems if a framework for the structure of the report can be agreed at the outset. It will also help the writer if there are individuals who can offer advice, support and discuss ideas while writing is in progress. A near final draft can then be circulated for comment.

If the profile has been a team effort, then the writing may also require a team approach. This has the advantage of maintaining the direct involvement of a wider group of people, allowing the sharing of skills and dividing the work into manageable sections. It is, however, essential that there is prior agreement about the form and content of the report, so as to produce a consistent and coherent final document. It is usually best to have one or two individuals who can bring all sections together to ensure consistency of style and eliminate any duplication. One should always

Figure 8.2   Guidelines for writing reports[3]

- Set deadlines for completion of discrete sections and the whole report
- Write regularly; assign a regular time and place to writing
- Keep up a rhythm of work; don't break off to chase up a reference
- Write up each section as soon as it is ready
- Stop at a point from which it is easy to resume
- Leave space for revision

bear in mind that collectively written reports are tied to the speed of the slowest writer. Figure 8.2 gives some basic tips on writing reports.

You will need to decide whether one single document can address all the issues and audiences simultaneously or whether the same material requires repackaging in different ways for different purposes. In many situations, it may be impractical to think of more than one written format, although a report with a leaflet summarizing the main results may be possible. However, the style and balance of a single report is particularly important. A document with unexplained acronyms (words formed from initials), academic jargon or technical terms may have its uses but is unlikely to have a wide readership among local people whose concerns are supposed to be reflected in the report. It is unlikely to be effective in rallying the local community to the call of the report.

The structure of a report

Before writing the report you will need a structure. Figure 8.3 gives an example of a typical report structure, which might be used as the basis for developing your own outline. In addition, you should go back to your project aims and objectives to remind yourself of the issues that the project was designed to address.

The *title page* should include the name of the report. You should think carefully about this. You might want to use a title that captures the imagination of those who the profile is aimed at. This might be a particularly telling phrase that has come out of the fieldwork or it might be a straightforward description of what it is. The annotated bibliography which appears at the end of this book gives examples of what others have called their reports. Many

Figure 8.3   Typical report structure

- Title page
- Summary
- Acknowledgements
- Contents page
- Introduction
- Body of report subdivided into appropriate sections
- Conclusions
- Recommendations
- References
- Appendices

reports have a general title followed by a more informative subtitle, for example 'A very welcome scheme: An evaluation of a childcare initiative in a local community'. The title page should also include the names of the authors of the report or the group which produced it, who published it and the date or year of publication.

Many reports begin with a brief *summary* of key points aimed at those people who do not have the time or interest to read the whole document. This might also provide the basis for a separate short document which might be circulated more widely. The summary should take the form of a series of points so that it can be read quickly. You should summarize Introduction, Methodology, Results as well as Conclusions and Recommendations.

While *acknowledgements* are not essential, it is important to thank all those people who contributed to the production of the community profile. This might include people in the community who attended discussion meetings or who were interviewed, those who undertook the fieldwork, or helped to deliver and collect questionnaires, those who entered data or did the analysis, the person or people who typed the report or contributed illustrations or helped put together an exhibition. It is very important that acknowledgements are comprehensive, correct (i.e. names spelt properly) and politically sensitive.

The *contents* page, especially in a long report, should include all headings and subheadings so that the reader can see easily where they need to look for information on a particular topic. It is also common practice to list tables and figures separately after the contents page.

In the *introduction*, you might want to include the background to the project (how it came about), the context of the report, the terms of reference and the aims and objectives of the profile. You should also give details about methodology (how the information was collected) to demonstrate the validity and reliability of your findings. If you have undertaken a survey you should give details about your sample – how it was derived, how representative it was – and the response rate. Where you have undertaken group discussions or meetings, explain how these were organized and structured.

The *body of the report* should provide details of findings from all stages of the community-profiling process organized by theme or topic into sections that follow on from each other in a logical fashion. Headings and sub-headings should act as signposts to the reader guiding them through the report.[4] Each chapter or section of the report should begin with an introduction indicating in broad terms the content, and should conclude with a brief summary of key points or issues.

The *conclusions* should follow logically from the findings in the body of the report but should not be used to introduce new information. The findings might be summarized, key issues identified and lead on to the *recommendations*. These should be succinct and flow from the findings and the conclusions. The recommendations are suggestions for action in light of the findings of the research. If there is a long list of recommendations, you may find it useful to group them by theme or according to the agencies to whom they are addressed. However, you may decide not to include recommendations until you have undertaken consultation over a local action plan (see Chapter 9).

Cluttering the text itself with detailed *references* to the sources you have used can make the text difficult to read. However, it is good practice to note the sources used, and this may be valuable for follow-up work. An annotated bibliography or 'Notes on sources' is more useful than a simple listing of references. Any book on report writing will give you information on how to write references.

Appendices normally contain technical information or copies of documents that it is inappropriate to include in the main part of the report. If you use secondary sources, then you should list them in the appendices. Any information-gathering tool that you have used such as a questionnaire or interview schedule could be included in the appendices. In addition, one could list groups, organizations and individuals contacted or interviewed. However, you need to check that individuals are happy that their names appear in the report. In general, people who have been interviewed as part of a survey should not be named. Any publicity material produced might also be included in the appendices.

Writing style

Most of the literature on report writing recommends that the KISS rule should be adhered to – keep it short and simple.[5] This approach is equally valid when writing a community profile. Another important consideration in the context of community profiles is ensuring that the statements that you make are warranted by your research findings. In other words, you should not make sweeping statements or generalizations that cannot be supported by any evidence: 'The use of facts in communication gives authority to statements and arguments'.[6] If you make a comment such as 'The whole community expressed the need for a purpose built community centre', then you must be able to substantiate that statement. Exaggerating your findings can damage the credibility of the profiling exercise as a whole. Figure 8.4 provides some general tips on writing style.

Collating information

In order to produce your community profile, you may have to bring together material from a wide range of different sources. These might include official publications, census data, statistics from the

Figure 8.4 General tips on writing style

- Use only as many words as are needed to make your point
- Choose familiar words; avoid jargon
- Be precise; avoid vague or ambiguous words and expressions
- Avoid cliches
- Use as little punctuation as possible
- Avoid slang words and expressions
- Check spelling
- Explain any abbreviations used

health authority, survey findings, material obtained from interviews with members of the community, service providers, policy makers and community representatives, and notes of group discussions or public meetings. You may also have maps and photographs and graphic representations of statistical information. Your report should attempt to integrate all these different kinds of information in a coherent way. Where different sources point to a similar conclusion, this should be referred to as it suggests that there is considerable evidence in support of it. Where this is not the case, for example where official perceptions do not agree with those of the community, then this should also be mentioned as it is an important finding of the research in its own right.

As has already been mentioned, statistical information on its own can often be difficult to digest. It is therefore a good idea to break up this type of information with other types. For example, you may want to use photographs to break up the text or verbatim quotes from in-depth interviews or group discussions that enliven the report and illuminate the points being made in the text and through the statistical information. However, it is important that the reader is always aware of the source of the information being presented.

You will need to be selective about what to include in your report. You will almost certainly have more information than you can use, so it is vital that only the most significant, relevant and telling information is put in, so that readers are not distracted by material which is peripheral or irrelevant.

Editing and proof-reading

Once you have produced a first draft of your community profile, you will face the tasks of editing and proof-reading in order to produce a final report that can be printed and circulated. The process of revising and rewriting a draft report often takes longer than one expects, as you now have the opportunity to reflect on what you have written and you will inevitably see better ways in which to organize and present your material. Where the first draft of the report has been written by a group of people, you will almost certainly need to get one person to act as editor in order to impose some uniformity of style. Figure 8.5 provides a checklist of issues to consider when editing a report.

Figure 8.5   Checklist of issues to consider during editing

- Is the material in the report in the right order?
- Is the general tone of the report appropriate to the intended audience?
- Is the report readable?
- Is the material presented clearly?
- Is it concise? Is every word and sentence necessary?
- Is it complete? Has anything been omitted?
- Are all statements and conclusions backed up by appropriate evidence?
- Is the information in the report correct?
- Can key issues be clearly identified?

Once the content of the report has been agreed through whatever methods of consultation that were decided upon, you can produce a final report which incorporates any amendments or additions made during the consultation stage. Before multiple copies are produced, this draft must be carefully proof-read to eliminate typing errors and spelling mistakes.

Desktop publisher, wordprocessor or typewriter?

People's expectations in relation to printed documents has risen sharply in recent years due to the increased availability of word-processing and desktop publishing packages. While the cheapest way of producing a report is probably still to type it on a typewriter and then photocopy and staple it, this will not result in a terribly professional looking document, especially if graphs are hand-written or lines on tables are drawn in.

Using a word-processing package and a good-quality printer will dramatically improve the appearance of your report and most are easy to use. However, desktop publishing (DTP) software packages are now increasingly common and many are available for less than £100. They can also considerably enhance the appearance of a finished document. However, they do have some disadvantages. DTP packages are not always easy to use and to make the most effective use of them requires some design skills.

Whichever method you use for producing your final copy, you will then have to consider how to produce multiple copies. If your final copy is of a high enough standard, then you can simply take it to a printer to produce the number of copies you require. If your copy is not to a high enough standard but you have produced it using a word processor, then you can save yourself a considerable amount of money by taking a disk containing the text of your report to a printer and asking for it to be printed to a higher quality or for a minimum amount of typesetting to be undertaken to improve the quality of your copy.

Design

'The first impact of a report or other working document makes does not depend on words'.[7] As this statement suggests, in order to persuade people to read your report you need to make it look attractive. This means that you have to give some attention to the layout and design of your material. In this section, we include some suggestions which you may wish to adopt.

One of the most important issues to consider is what is it like to read the text of the report? Is each page crammed full of small type that looks very daunting and is difficult to read? Research has found that a line length of 52–72 characters or approximately 10–12 words per line is a comfortable length to read. If the line is too short or too long, then it will make the process of reading more difficult. The space between lines is also important. If lines are too close together, reading will be more difficult. The eyes of the reader will be strained if the type you are using is small and the characters are almost touching.

Can headings be clearly distinguished from the rest of the text? Primary headings should be in a different typeface (e.g. capitals or italics) and possibly a different size and secondary headings should be different again.

Another important aspect of design is the cover of your report. It is worth spending some time and resources on producing an attractive design for the cover. After all, although the content of the report is the main thing, it is also important to encourage people to pick it up and read it. Whether you use an illustration, graphics or just words, your aim should be to produce something that is eye-catching, attractive and well-designed but that is also relevant to the subject matter of the report. The cover should convey, in general terms, what the report is about.

Key issues

The way in which you collate and present the material gathered during the community-profiling process can affect the effectiveness with which you communicate the key issues to emerge from your research. Effective communication depends on an understanding of the information which you wish to communicate and empathy with those with whom you are trying to communicate. While community profiles can make use of a number of different means of communication, most will involve the production of a written report.

To be effective, a written report must present information in a way that is easy to read and easy to understand. These objectives can be achieved by ordering material in a logical and coherent manner, using language that is simple and appropriate to the intended readership, making good use of different kinds of information to enliven the text and by giving sufficient attention to page layout and overall design. While DTP can considerably enhance the appearance of a document, a word-processing package should be sufficient to produce an attractive report.

Further reading

Chapman, M. (1986) *Plain Figures*. London: HMSO.
Collier, D. (1991) *Collier's Rules for Desktop Design and Typography*. Wokingham: Addison-Wesley.
Cuba, L. (1993) *A Short Guide to Writing about Social Science*, 2nd edn. New York: Harper Collins.
Fletcher, J. (1983) *How to Write a Report*. London: Institute of Personnel Management.
Gowers, E. (1962) *The Complete Plain Words*. Harmondsworth: Pelican.

Notes

1. Orna, E. and Stevens, G. (1991) 'Information design and information science: A new alliance', *Journal of Information Science*, Vol. 17, pp. 197–208.
2. Ellis, R. and Hopkins, K. (1985) *How to Succeed in Written Work and Study*. Glasgow: Collins.
3. Bell, J. (1993) *Doing your research project*, 2nd edn, p. 125. Buckingham: Open University Press.
4. Chapman, M. (1986) *Plain Figures*, p. 93. London: HMSO.

5. Wells, G. (1991) *Everyone's Business on Effective Communication*, p. 11. Singapore: EFB Publishers.
6. Eyre, E.C. (1979) *Effective Communication Made Simple*, p. 25. London: W.H. Allen.
7. Fletcher, J. (1983) *How to Write a Report*, p. 27. London: Institute of Personnel Management.

9
Not the end

Introduction

Primary and secondary information has been gathered, collated and analysed; the community's needs have been assessed and resources audited; problems and issues have been identified; and a report or some other summary of your findings has been prepared. So what happens next? The production of the profile should not be considered as the end of the process. In order for the completed community profile to have an impact, at least two things have to happen. First, the profile has to be publicized and circulated so that the information enters the public domain. And, second, strategies have to be developed that address the issues identified by the profiling exercise.

In this chapter, we examine some of the ways that you might go about publicizing the profile before moving on to explore possible ways in which the profile might be used. Finally, we conclude by looking at the implications of having done a community profile and the ways in which the initial research might be followed up in the longer term.

Publicizing the profile

In considering how to go about publicizing and advertising the availability of the completed community profile, you will need to consider who you want to take note of it. The first group who should be informed of the profile is the community itself. The profile is about them; they contributed to the findings; and any action that results is likely to affect them. There is therefore an argument to say that morally they collectively *own* the profile and therefore have a right to know what it contains. However, it is important

also to notify all those who contributed in any way to the profile.
This might include:

- members of the community;
- community and voluntary organizations;
- councillors / MPs;
- interested professionals; and
- statutory agencies.

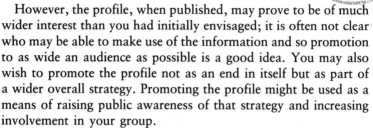

However, the profile, when published, may prove to be of much
wider interest than you had initially envisaged; it is often not clear
who may be able to make use of the information and so promotion
to as wide an audience as possible is a good idea. You may also
wish to promote the profile not as an end in itself but as part of
a wider overall strategy. Promoting the profile might be used as a
means of raising public awareness of that strategy and increasing
involvement in your group.

Chapter 3 stressed the need for publicity at various stages
throughout the profiling process, from the very early stages
through to the final report. Publicity not only helps to ensure a high
level of community involvement and to maximize participation, but
also provides a means of obtaining feedback about the profile's
findings. Now that the profile is finished, it might be an appropriate time to go to the community once again to present the report
before it is used for any of the applications explored later.

How to promote the community profile

Once the reasons for promoting the profile are clearer and the
target audience has been decided on, you can determine the range
of methods that are most appropriate for getting the findings
across. It cannot be assumed that because you have found the profile and its contents riveting that everyone else will do so. In the
last chapter, we looked at ways of making the profile as attractive
as possible to readers. You can also make it more difficult to ignore
by using one or more of the publicity methods described in this
section.

Most of these methods are complementary to each other and,
if used in conjunction with one another, will contribute to the
overall effectiveness. An exhibition, for example, will gain a wider
audience if well publicized with leaflets and a press release. It is,
therefore, a good idea to organize a full launch of the profile using

as many methods as possible. Here we look at a range of methods involving (1) some form of written communication that is circulated to the appropriate people, (2) activities or events to draw further attention to the profile and (3) taking the profile to your target audiences.

Written publicity is of primary importance in promoting your profile. Press releases are one of the first forms of publicity to consider. Personal contact with known reporters is best and can help to ensure that the key issues that you want to get across are fully understood. You should send a copy of the full report, if practical, although the significant points should also be emphasized in the press release. Press releases should be sent to all local papers – daily, evening and weekly free newspapers. They may also be picked up by the local radio for their community slots, and occasionally local television stations.

Leaflets notifying people about the profile or any events promoting it might also be produced. You should try to keep these simple, although they should include the key issues to have emerged from the profile. It is useful to say who produced the profile, which community it is about, where copies of the complete report can be obtained and how much they cost. It is often a good idea to incorporate the cover design of the report. You might also want to include a tear-off slip for ordering copies of the report.

Posters are another form of local publicity. In order to have much impact, posters need to be eye-catching in order to gain the interest of casual passers-by. If advertising a launch or event, don't forget to include time, date and venue. Make sure someone proofreads it before having it printed.

The report itself may be rather long and not easily accessible to the 'ordinary' reader. In these circumstances, it is advisable to prepare a summary of the report with clear, easily understandable graphics which can be handed out to a wider audience. A summary such as this need be no more than four to six sides of A4 with 'bullet points' emphasizing the key issues. Where a commitment has been made to inform the whole community of the findings of the report, a summarized version such as this may be produced relatively cheaply with a photocopier and circulated perhaps as a newsletter to all members of the community.[1] Many communities have their own newsletters produced by a community centre, community association, parish council or church. Most will be only too pleased to include an article, or even a series of articles, about the findings of the profile.

After producing some initial written publicity, you may want to consider *staging an event* such as a public meeting or a series of meetings. These have the advantage of fulfilling a number of functions. The findings can be presented; key speakers (perhaps from agencies who might wish to address needs that have been identified) can be invited to respond to the issues raised; questions and discussions with the community can take place; and action can be planned.

You might either hold a one-off meeting, perhaps to launch the profile, or a series of smaller meetings, possibly more locally based, where discussion can take place more informally. An alternative approach is to organize several meetings, each addressing a different theme or issue such as the needs of the elderly or environmental problems. A number of events might be organized in conjunction with each other to form a community festival. This might include formal speeches or presentations from community leaders, councillors, MPs or representatives from agencies responsible for service delivery. It might include an exhibition and a series of workshops exploring the different issues that have been highlighted in the profile.[2] You might want to invite other community groups to provide stalls or activities that promote their organizations.

Finally, if people have not been informed about the profile as a result of these activities, then you might want to *take your message to them*. This can be tackled in a number of ways. Having prepared leaflets, summary reports and possibly exhibition boards, you need to find appropriate venues to which to take them. Local groups such as Women's Institutes and establishments such as sheltered housing complexes are often looking for speakers; schools are usually keen for pupils to become involved in the community; or there may be local fetes or events where a stall can be set up. Agencies such as the local social services and housing offices may be interested to hear the views of members of the community and may be willing to have a presentation at a team meeting or exhibition boards in waiting rooms. Many town halls will host an exhibition which is of local interest. You may also be able to take part in other community events such as summer fetes.

Beyond publicity

The profile has now been produced, everyone with a special interest has been informed and the profile has had maximum publicity. Your group may now have fulfilled its objectives and may wish to disband. However, that is hopefully not the end of the profile; in many ways it is only the start. In publicizing the findings of the profile, you may have created a demand for further action. Issues will have been highlighted and discussed and possible recommendations made. If the project group feels that its job is now finished, there are a number of possible courses of action.

At public meetings and similar events, people will have been made aware of the issues and possibilities. Some may now wish to form an action committee to progress the recommendations. That group could, depending on the issues, focus on one problem or a cluster of concerns; or perhaps more than one group may evolve, focusing on different aspects of the findings. It is a good idea, when organizing final promotional meetings of the profile, to try to have available experts who can help give advice and practical support for anyone wishing to take the issues further. There may also be organizations already in existence, such as community groups, which are willing to pursue the issues.

What happens after the completion of a community profile is not always predictable. The next section looks at a range of possible applications of a community profile and potential developments from it.

Principal applications

Twenty years ago, one of the authors undertook a community profile of an inner-city community as part of a placement with an independent youth and community work agency. Like many such projects, the principal aim was to gather information. However, the agency was interested in the profile and it became part of its information system. What this example shows is that even profiles with no explicit purpose beyond that of gathering information may also serve other functions. In this case, the profile was not only a valuable learning experience, but was also of use to other workers in the community who used the information gained to inform and plan the delivery of their future work. It also created greater self-awareness within the community itself.

Gathering, collating and presenting information about a community is a means to several possible ends. Those ends may not fall neatly into one or other of the following categories; they may cover several or all of them. However, we will examine three principal uses for community profiles which, when viewed in this way, may prove valuable when considering both the initial stages of planning a profile and also identifying the way forward once it is completed. The first is simply to provide a valuable source of information about the community. Second, community profiling can contribute to more effective service provision, policy planning and evaluation. And, third, community profiles can be used as part of a broader community development strategy.

Providing a source of valuable information

If a community profile is being undertaken as a means to other ends, then it becomes important to clearly specify and understand those ends, or uses, in order to determine what information needs to be collated and the format in which it is to be stored and presented. Many profiles, however, are actually undertaken solely in the expectation that information gathered might be of use in the future. Additionally, information that emerges in the course of undertaking a profile is sometimes not foreseeable, and a totally open and eclectic aim of gathering information at the start can produce interesting results.

Collecting information about communities for others to use has been the province of libraries and librarians for some time. In their study of profiles and public libraries, Jordan and Walley quote one librarian who said that they use profiles 'to ensure the library has all the answers which might be asked about the community'. They also found that 'Camden, probably because it receives more visitors and students on placement than most libraries, found profiles especially useful for distributing to visiting students and librarians who require a background knowledge of Camden libraries'.[3] Community associations, parish councils and other campaigning bodies also find it useful to have a stock of knowledge about their locality and community which can provide facts, numbers and views for their members.

Profiles which aim to collate and distribute information in this way are not just one-off projects to be completed by a particular date and produced in a set written format. They should be

developed as an on-going enquiry-based data service that can produce printed fact sheets, guides or bulletins as required. Profiles
such as this will, of course, need constant updating as the community changes, and therefore methods of storage as well as production should reflect this need.[4]

A basis for developing and improving a service

Community profiles can be of use in the planning and delivery of
services at three points in the policy process. The first is the policy
formulation stage when an action plan or strategy is developed
which identifies the range of issues that need addressing based on
detailed knowledge of the community, along with a range of solutions for the issues identified. The second is in the implementation
of programmes and the delivery of services which are appropriate
to the needs of the community, and the third is the evaluation of
the outcomes of the policy and monitoring of the impact of policy
change on communities.

A community profile can be an essential first step in the process
of developing a plan of action to improve the well-being of a community by identifying the needs of that community, existing
resources and priorities for action. It is important that the issues
identified in the community profile be placed in context and that
your conclusions can be fully justified. Issues should be clearly
based on the findings of the community profile, both in terms of
the needs and the resources identified. However, you may also
want to compare levels of need and resources in your community
with the average for the wider community or include endorsement
of the priorities identified from experts or specialist organizations.

You will probably have identified a range of different issues
which will need to be addressed separately and in concert. Options
need to be presented and developed giving consideration to such
factors as:

• specification of targets where appropriate;
• identification of agencies/individuals responsible;
• details of specific costs; and
• indication of time-scale necessary for achieving targets.

The priorities for action identified at this stage must also be
realistic. It is very easy to get carried away developing plans which
have little regard for the realities of resource and time constraints.

While some imaginative and creative thinking is necessary, innovative ideas should be shaped to fit the actual circumstances.

At this stage, the set of priorities arrived at should attract a degree of consensus. A full assessment of community needs can help create that consensus among the relevant agencies, groups and individuals. Even if the action plan focuses on a single problem, it is likely that it will touch on a range of different issues and therefore necessitate a diversity of solutions and agencies.[5] If, for example, you have identified a lack of resources for children under five, you may need to involve all the following agencies in the search for solutions: social services (who register child-minders and creche facilities); health visitors (who often assist in forming parent and toddler groups); the housing department (which may own property that can be of use); the leisure department (which may provide play facilities); and other agencies which have a specialist interest such as the police, the Pre-school Playgroup Association, Gingerbread and so on.

It is crucial, therefore, that if the community profile is intended to form the basis for a local action plan, then all relevant agencies should become involved from the start of the process, thereby developing the necessary comprehensive, multi-agency approach to the resolution of issues and to the meeting of needs.

It is also important that even people who are not actively involved in the development of the action plans are broadly in support of them. Action plans should ideally command the support not only of all relevant agencies but also of the community as well. The profiling process is a valuable way of informing and involving residents in the planning and implementation of action plans (see also Chapter 3). Community leaders and representatives should certainly be involved at this stage, as they may provide the political clout necessary to push the action plan through.

The second part of the policy process where community profiles can play a part is implementation. Accurate information about the communities which are on the receiving end of services will help to ensure that the ways in which services are delivered are appropriate to the particular needs of those communities, contributing to the overall effectiveness of those services.

In recent years, both statutory and voluntary agencies have become increasingly concerned about the quality of the services they provide. Moves to provide a better quality service have often materialized as changes in the way in which services are delivered, such as:

- decentralization;
- inter-agency cooperation;
- service user participation; and
- citizen consultation.

Social services and housing departments have typically led the way in taking their offices into local communities, making them more accessible and more responsive to the needs of local residents. Some local authorities, such as Islington, have gone further and established 'one-stop-shops', which provide a wide range of services in one locally based building. Most of those who are responsible for establishing local offices will agree that an essential element in the process is that of understanding the real issues and needs within the community served, and community profiles are one way of achieving that understanding.

Most issues affecting communities necessitate a wide range of solutions involving a number of different agencies and departments. Bringing these agencies and departments together is therefore important not just at the planning stage but also in the practical business of providing services to the community. Community profiling, as we have seen, can contribute to the development of a consensus on issues and priorities among different agencies.

'Consulting the customers' and 'learning from the community' are typical of the new approach being developed in public services. There is a growing belief by public sector agencies in the importance of finding out what people think of current forms of service delivery and how they might be improved. Furthermore, as we saw in Chapter 1, community consultation has become a requirement of a number of central government initiatives such as Neighbourhood Renewal Assessments, Estate Action and City Challenge. This approach is partly based on the recognition that professionals and politicians do not necessarily know what people want or need, and if services are to be developed that are appropriate to those needs, appropriate methods must be used to identify them. Many consultations with service users tend to be 'market research' studies, although community profiling could provide much richer information. Consulting the public goes a long way towards providing valuable information for providers of services and can indicate to people that their views are valued. However, customer consultations are only a part of what could be seen as 'real' citizen participation. Participation is about giving people a real voice in the planning and running of services, and allowing them to take more control over those aspects of their life or environment.

Participation starts with a two-way process of sharing information and opinions, which may take the form of satisfaction surveys, information leaflets, newsletters, or through a full community profile. However, it is important that such exercises are not perceived by the community as cosmetic exercises undertaken primarily for political or propaganda purposes. People's expectations may be raised unnecessarily and the community's feelings that they are the passive recipient of services reinforced. Participation should seek to actively involve citizens in the decision-making process, to find ways of enabling them to at least influence, if not make, decisions. This means including them fully in the planning as well as implementation stages.

Finally, an important aspect of the policy process is the monitoring of the impact of policy and evaluating outcomes. The information derived from a community-profiling exercise can provide a benchmark against which progress can be measured. In developing a community action plan to address issues identified by the profile, a strategy for monitoring and evaluation should also be developed. That monitoring and evaluation should relate to the aims and objectives identified in the action plan and appropriate targets set. In addition, a standard format for undertaking profiles provides the possibility of making detailed comparisons between areas or groups in relation to their needs and levels of resource allocation. This is important not only in targeting resources as discussed above, but also in relation to evaluation.

Advancing the community's cause

The third major use that you can put your profile to is in assisting the community. In Chapter 3, we looked at involving communities in profiling their community and examined the relationship between residents and the people who work with, and seek to help, them. Here we show how both the process of undertaking a community profile and the profile itself can be useful to those seeking to improve the well-being of the community.

Figure 9.1　Community development

The goal is self help and the integration of community groups. The task is to create total community ignoring class cleavages. It is assumed that there are common interests among different groups. The centre strategy is directed towards achieving communication between them.

(DHSS 1982)

Three broad approaches to community work have been identified by observers and researchers of community-based work. These were summarized in a survey carried out for the Department of Health and Social Security[6] as:

- community development (see Fig. 9.1);
- community action (see Fig. 9.2); and
- community planning (see Fig. 9.4).

In the work of any community worker, or other person working within the community and assisting local development, all three types of approaches may be used, and, similarly, a community profile may serve to assist the community in any or all three.

Where the aim of a community profile is largely to assist in the development of that community, the emphasis may be less on the product and more on the processes it entails. As we saw in Chapter 3, community profiling can act as a very powerful tool in encouraging motivation, bringing people together, generating community involvement, building confidence and raising awareness, as well as identifying both problems and opportunities.

Community profiling has been used as a tool to facilitate and inform the work of community workers and as a process that can be adopted by other professions since the early 1950s in the USA (see Chapter 3). In Britain, too, community profiling has been seen as invaluable for informing the work of local professionals, especially those starting fresh in an area. The following advice was given in a social work manual. 'It is probably useful if, soon after starting work in an area . . . the worker puts on paper his impressions of the current population. [It] should help to clarify ideas about possible courses of action. It may also be helpful to refer back to it later to see what problems that struck one initially one has later neglected or were incorrectly assessed'.[7] Similarly, Twelvetrees, in a more recent book wrote:

The purpose of a community profile is first, to gather information about the needs of a locality and the potential for action and second, to provide the basis for an analysis of possible alternative courses of action from which to choose priorities. In the process of gathering the relevant information you will make contact with many people, and some of those contacts are likely to be the starting-point for action.[8]

Profiles are not only of use to workers when commencing work in a particular area; they also provide a mechanism whereby those involved can begin to understand the background and basis on which their community operates. Knowledge about the history, cultural setting and local economic structure, all add greatly to the sense of identity and social cohesion experienced in a community. Also, undertaking the tasks of collecting and analysing the information that profiling brings allows participants to interpret their immediate circumstances in a new way.

Community profiles are sometimes used by members of a community to provide ammunition for a particular campaign for better services, improved conditions, resources for a need that is not currently being met, against a particular development or for more participation in the provision of those services. It may be that specific issues highlighted in the report give cause for concern or an existing group already involved in work on that issue wish to undertake a profile to emphasize their case. Findings from the profile can be fed into official channels (mainly statutory but also larger voluntary organizations) to inform policy formulation, implementation and evaluation.

An example of how one group formed around the problems of living in their 1960s high-rise flats and maisonettes, conducted a survey and publicized it is given in Fig. 9.3.

Figure 9.2 Community action

> The goal is a change in power relationships and resources. The clientele are disadvantaged sections of the community. The practice is to help them to be organised, to crystallise action issues and to engage in conflict against power structures.
>
> (DHSS, 1982)

Figure 9.3   The Cartmell Drive Exhibition Group

The following excerpts are taken from a book written by a group
of council tenants, which chronicles their campaign to achieve better
housing standards. It illustrates many of the techniques and processes that are described in this chapter.

> We called ourselves the "Cartmell Drive Exhibition Group",
> and our main aim was to highlight the plight of the people
> living in system built housing in the area, but to put it over
> in such a way that it would stand out in people's minds . . .
> It was finally agreed that we would do this by staging an
> exhibition, containing information on our findings, photo-
> graphs and a video . . .
>   There followed a year of frustration, hard work, dis-
> appointments, sleepless nights of worry, letter writing, attend-
> ing classes, learning how to make a video, doing surveys,
> raking up as much information as we could get . . . Much was
> learnt from this process. Several people from other Tenant's
> Associations did become involved in varying degrees . . .
>   Despite a last minute rush, our exhibition opened on time.
> Sandra Clarkson [a tenant] made the opening speech and
> introduced Derek Fatchett M.P., who was officially to open
> our exhibition. Several councillors attended, also many pro-
> fessionals who worked in the area or were interested in
> this issue came, and the opening was well covered by local

The most distinctive role that community-profiling techniques
can play within community planning is that of compiling direc-
tories of local resources and services. Knowledge about the area in
which you work is invaluable in providing a flexible, comprehensive and sensitive service, as we have seen in this chapter. Community profiles can also be used as the basis for inter-agency or
inter-departmental working. Information is collected across the
range of community, statutory and voluntary organizations, and
can be shared between them. Issues, needs and concerns will cross-
cut the boundaries of the various agencies and so auditing them will
provide a suitable opportunity for these residents and workers to
collectively seek solutions.

Figure 9.3 Continued

> television and radio stations and the local press. Overall it
> went very well and most people seemed impressed.
>   From then on all sorts of things have happened to us. We
> were invited to show our exhibition and video at the next full
> council meeting. Mr Fatchett arranged for Sandra and Barbara
> [Barbara Young was a tenant and co-author of the book] to
> meet the then Housing Minister, Ian Gow, in London. Bar-
> bara went again to London (to visit other tenants groups and
> have a meeting with the Building Research Establishment).
>   [Final note by Barbara]: Derek Fatchett phoned me and
> asked me to arrange a meeting, he said that the reports would
> be ready by then, and that he and our councillors wanted to
> tell us before any-one else. This meeting was one that I will
> never forget. We had won, just like that! A pilot scheme was
> to be looked at with the view to strengthening one of the
> blocks if it could be done. We were congratulated and praised
> and thanked for our efforts.
>   I can't properly describe how I feel; to say that I feel proud
> might sound pompous. I think the best thing to say is that in
> some ways we have shown that ordinary people – "tenants",
> can bring about changes for the better if they have the deter-
> mination to work at it.
>   *Yesterday's Dream – Today's Nightmare*
>   (The Cartmell Drive Exhibition Group 1987)

Figure 9.4 Community planning

> It has as its focus problem solving in regard to substantive social
> problems. Clientele are made up of consumers or recipients of ser-
> vices. Either consensus or conflict may be used as a strategy. A basic
> assumption is that change can be brought about by rational decision
> making.
>   (DHSS 1982)

Keeping in touch with the profile

Producing the profile, in whatever form, may be the final stage for
the profiling group. However, you may still have a longer-term
interest in the profile and how it is used. Your group may wish to

remain together in some form in order to monitor the longer-term outcomes of the profile and to update it when necessary. At the very least, it is useful to come together again a year after the profile has been launched in order to assess any impact that it has had on the community in that period. It can be very encouraging and rewarding to record improvements made as a result of your efforts. However, many changes take a long time to take effect. You may also want to look at why things are not happening as quickly as you had hoped, in which areas there has been noticeable change, and what the outstanding issues are. Is there a need for further publicity, lobbying or other action? Were there omissions in the profile that have now come to light? Changes, however, can occur more rapidly, and within five years or so you may decide that there is a need to repeat the whole exercise. Certainly many things will have changed in this time.

Key issues

The community profile you have planned, for which you have brought people together to discuss and organize, gather information for, analyse data and spend so much time and effort writing up and producing, is now ready. It is now time to let people know about your findings. Having decided who you want to tell, you have to decide what is the most appropriate method of telling them. This chapter provides some suggestions as to how you might go about doing this.

However, this is still not the end of the story. You will also need to decide what to do with the profile and how you might best make use of the information it contains. There are a number of possible uses. Those that we have examined in this chapter are: to provide a set of interesting and informative facts to place in the public domain; to assist in the process of policy formulation and implementation with the aim of improving the quality and relevance of local services; and to contribute to the process of community development, action and planning. If citizens are to take an active part in the running of their community, they need the information, skills and awareness that undertaking a community profile can bring. In practice, you are likely to want to embrace more than one of these applications, the uses of which are partly dependent on who employs the profile, whether that is directly by residents groups, other local organizations, agency workers or a combination of all these interested parties.

Finally, as we said at the start of this chapter, this is *not the end*. Profiling a community can be a continuous process, constant updating and checking can keep it relevant, and constantly reviewing the results can ensure that it becomes a success. We hope, however, that after having undertaken the profile in the ways we suggest, involving as many members of the community as possible and using a wide range of techniques, you will have found it not only rewarding but also a very enjoyable experience. If so, undertaking future profiles should be equally enjoyable.

Further reading

Bird, P. (1992) *How to Run a Local Campaign*. Plymouth: How to Books.

Bryson, J.M. (1988) *Strategic Planning for Public Service and Non-Profit Organisations*. Oxford: Pergamon Press.

Bryson, J.M. (ed.) (1992) *Strategic Planning for Public Service and Non-Profit Organisations*. San Francisco, CA: Jossey-Bass.

Cartmell Drive Exhibition Group (1987) *Yesterday's Dream – Today's Nightmare*. Leeds: Cartmell Drive Exhibition Group.

Gibson, T. (1977) 'Planning for Real'. In *Neighbourhood Action Packs*. Nottingham: Neighbourhood Initiatives Foundation.

Jones, M. (1992) *Using the Media*. London: Bedford Square Press.

Lowndes, B. (1990) *Getting Your Message Across*. London: NFCO.

Notes

1. See *Bloomsbury Safety Audit* (Safe Estates for Women 1992) for an example of the production of a summarized version of a report.
2. For an example of how a group can use a variety of publicity methods, see the Cartmell Drive Exhibition Group (1987) in Fig. 9.3.
3. Jordan, P. and Walley, E. (1977) *Learning about the Community: A Guide for Public Librarians*. Leeds: Leeds Polytechnic.
4. A number of the profiles listed in the Annotated Bibliography provide illustrations of the ways in which agencies use profiles to provide information.
5. See, e.g. Bowling, A. (1990) 'Associations with life satisfaction among very elderly people living in a deprived part of inner London', *Social Science Medicine*, Vol. 1, pp. 1002–1011; *Accident Prevention: Child Protection – A Community Approach* (Roberts 1991).
6. Department of Health and Social Security (1982) *Local Authority Community Work: Realities of Practice*. London: HMSO.

7. Baldock, P. (1974) *Community Work and Social Work*. London: Routledge and Kegan Paul.
8. Twelvetrees, A. (1982) *Community Work*. London: British Association of Social Workers/Macmillan.

Annotated bibliography

This bibliography aims to provide information about other groups/organizations working in the field of community profiling and the methods they have employed. As can be seen from the structure of the bibliography, reports have been gathered from a number of sources: citizens' advice bureaux, church groups, community action agencies, health authorities/community health councils, independent consultants, local authorities, political activists, self-study groups, universities/polytechnics/colleges and others. Yet it is not a comprehensive collection, neither in terms of geographical spread (profiles from Northern Ireland are yet to be collected), nor in the range of authors covered (it is particularly difficult to obtain profiles carried out by self-study groups). We aim to rectify this by continuing to collect as wide a selection of profiles as possible, to be added to our database through which further contacts can be developed. If you know of any profile not listed in the bibliography, please send details and a copy of the profile report if available to:

Policy Research Unit
16 Queen Square
Leeds LS2 8AJ

We hope this, and future bibliographies, will contribute to ideas and contacts between all kinds of groups across the country, providing stimulus for further work in this area.

Profiles by Citizens Advice Bureaux (CABs)

Report: Kensington and Chelsea Citizens Advice Bureau (1992) *Kensington and Chelsea Profile*. London: Kensington and Chelsea CAB.

Contact information: National Association of Citizens Advice Bureaux (NCAB: tel. 071 8332181).
Aims of study: To fulfil conditions of membership to CAB.
Methods: Gathering of statistics on the borough. Sources included: Department of Education and Science, Office of Population, Census and Surveys (OPCS), Policy Studies Institute, Riverside Health Authority and the Borough of Kensington and Chelsea.
General comments: Considered by NCAB to be a good model for other CABs to follow.

Report: Richmond Citizens Advice Bureau (1992) *Community Profile*. London: Richmond CAB.
Contact information: National Association of Citizens Advice Bureaux (NCAB: tel. 071 8332181).
Aims of study: To compile a profile to enable Richmond CAB to comply with NCAB standards for membership.
Methods: Unknown. Secondary sources included: OPCS, LRC and Richmond Borough Council.
General comments: No bibliography or methods.

Profiles by church groups

Report: Cross Gates Council of Churches (1989) *Report of the Mission Audit Group of the Cross Gates Council of Churches*. Leeds: Cross Gates Council of Churches
Contact information: Rev. John Holmes (tel. 0532 645530).
Aims of study: A community needs assessment to demonstrate church commitment to a caring neighbourhood.
Methods: Primary sources: a street survey and a congregational survey using a questionnaire and a door-to-door survey of two contrasting estates. Analysis using SPSSX.

Report: Roundhay Community of Churches (1989) *The Brackenwood Survey '89: 'A Community in Charge'*. Leeds: Roundhay Community of Churches.
Contact information: Rev. Jackie Treetops, St Edmunds Parish Church, Lidgett Park Road, Leeds LS8 1JN.
Size of study: An estate of 926 households.
Aims of study: To assess the needs of the estate, particularly transport, shopping and community facilities.
Methods: Primary sources: a household questionnaire administered by trained volunteers.

Report: St. Mathias Anglican and Burley Methodist Churches (1988) *Burley 1988 – A Parish Survey*. Leeds: St Mathias Anglican and Burley Methodist Churches.
Contact information: Rev. Howard Smith (tel. 0532 783666).
Size of study: 100 residents.
Aims of study: To find out who lives in the parish, what happens there and what there is to get involved in?
Methods: Primary sources: a structured questionnaire administered to local people about the history and demography of Burley, transport, education, health and social services, special needs, recreation, politics, religion and attitudes to the area.
General comments: A well done local survey.

Report: Shiner, P. (1991) *The Cry of the People of Buttershaw*. Leeds: CANA.
Contact information: CANA, 51a Cardigan Road, Leeds.
Size of study: 150 + respondents.
Aims of study: Profile of the community and the role of the church.
Methods: Primary sources: semi-structured interviews, questionnaire with local residents, professionals, church-goers, school groups; observation/walkabout. Secondary sources: local statistics.

Profiles by community action groups

Research: Griffiths, L. *et al.* (1988) *Communities Under the Hammer: Privy to Privatization*. Castleford. Yorkshire Art Circus.
Contact information: Yorkshire Art Circus (tel. 0977 550401).
Aims of study: To show every community has a story to tell.
Methods: Stories and photographs collected from interviews in South Elmsall Library, the Grove Community Centre and other community groups.

Research: Hulme, J. (1986) *A Photographic Memory*. Castleford: Yorkshire Art Circus.
Contact information: Yorkshire Art Circus (tel. 0977 550401).
Aims of study: To publish photographs of a Yorkshire mining town taken over a sixty-year period to provide a social history account.
Methods: Collection of over 9000 negatives representing life in Fryston, together with the photographer's memories of his life in the town.
General comments: Consists mainly of photographs.

Research: Moss, L. (1979) *Live and Learn – A Life of Struggle for Progress*. Brighton: Queenspark Books.
Contact information: Queenspark Books (tel. 0273 571916).
Size of study: One person.
Aims of study: To describe the author's life-story and the socio-political and economic change he has experienced; to gather support for victims of medical incompetence and promote 'area unionism'.
Methods: Tape-recording of conversations between the author and members of Queenspark; transcripts taken together with other documents to form a book. The author and Queenspark formed the editorial team, which continued to discuss issues from the text until the final draft was ready.

Research: Queenspark (1987) *Brighton on the Rocks*. Brighton: Queenspark Books.
Contact information: Queenspark Books (tel. 0273 571916).
Aims of study: To study the effects of monetarism on council service provision.
Methods: Interviews with local people who have experienced the direct effects of cuts in service provision.

Profiles by health authorities and community health councils

Report: Betts, G. (1985) *Health in Glydon*. London: Greenwich Community Health Council.
Contact information: Greenwich Community Health Council (tel. 081 3179994).
Size of study: 88 interviews.
Aims of study: To identify inequalities of health and ways to improve people's health via the provision of services to reflect the views of Glydon Ward.
Methods: Discuss and evaluate current services to find ways of improving them. Primary sources: interviews in the home using questions taken from the GHS and Nottingham Profile.

Report: Bowling, A. (1990) 'Associations with life satisfaction among very elderly people living in a deprived part of inner London', *Social Science Medicine*, Vol. 1, pp. 1002–1011.

Contact information: Ann Bowling, City and Hackney Health Authority (tel. 071 6064790).

Size of study: 662 people.

Aims of study: To determine the impact of social networks and support, functional status and reported mobility and life satisfaction.

Methods: Primary sources: interviews with people aged 85 and over living at home to ascertain their life circumstances, emotional well-being, mental and physical health status. Multiple regression analysis was used.

Report: City Challenge Health Project (1992) *City Challenge Health Project*. Birmingham: City Challenge Health Project.

Contact information: City Challenge Health Project (tel. 0902 314018).

Aims of study: To improve the health of the population in a deprived inner-city area.

Methods: Use of a community development model, looking at the causal problems of health and setting small, more easily attainable targets for health gain using consultation, Healthy Alliances, targeted/focused initiatives to empower residents and support of focus groups/self-help groups.

Report: Flatt, G.E. (1991) *A Study of the Area of Kirkstall and Hawksworth Wood – The Health Requirements of the Area*. Leeds.

Aims of study: To assess the relationship between the theoretical and health needs of a community while considering the stereotyping of ethnic minorities when providing health care.

Methods: Review of secondary data from city housing department, census, OPCS, health journals, Leeds Western Health Authority and Townsend P. Primary sources: an observational audit of the area.

General comments: Largely a literature-based study; no interviews with local people or service providers.

Report: Kirkstall Clinic (1990) *Community Profile of Kirkstall and Hawksworth*. Leeds: Kirkstall Clinic.

Aims of study: To increase health professionals' awareness of the community.

Methods: Combine knowledge of the staff and increase it via the compilation of secondary data from the health services and local planning department.

Report: Leeds Eastern Community Health Council (1990) *Health Matters in South Leeds*. Leeds: Leeds City CHC.
Contact information: Mike Simpkin, Health Liaison Officer (tel. 0532 457461).
Size of study: 1538 questionnaires posted.
Aims of study: To discover the views of South Leeds residents about health services, environment and lifestyle. Use the survey to contact local communities to create a network of local groups.
Methods: Primary sources: a general postal survey of one per cent of the population of South Leeds randomly selected from the electoral register. Provide small grants to local groups to carry out their own health-related projects. Further meetings plus feedback of project results plus local activities to groups in the area.
General comments: The project recognized the shortcomings of a postal questionnaire.

Report: Leeds Western Community Health Council (1987) *Leeds 12 Health Survey*. Leeds: Leeds Western CHC.
Contact information: Leeds Western CHC (tel. 0532 457461).
Size of study: 1000 individuals.
Aims of study: To find out about access to health services, the range of health services used and the public's view of the services.
Methods: Primary sources: a pilot survey and a postal survey which received a 49 per cent response rate.

Report: Leeds Western Community Health Council (1987) *Meeting Health Needs*. Leeds: Leeds Western CHC.
Contact information: Lyn Eckroyd, Bradford and Ilkley Community College (tel. 0274 753111).
Size of study: 22 respondents.
Aims of study: To investigate experience of black and ethnic minority women when coming into contact with general practitioners and hospital services.
Methods: Face-to-face interviews with women from ethnic minorities attending local classes.
General comments: Also contains information upon gaining access and undertaking such a survey.

Profiles by independent consultants

Report: Chisholm, N. (1989) *Economic Profile of Frizinghall Area, Bradford*. London: Community Economy Ltd.
Contact information: Community Economy Ltd (tel. 071 5196447).
Size of study: 240 households – a 15 per cent sample of the 1600 households in the area.
Aims of study: To identify community-based activities to occupy an extension to community centre and get a clearer picture of socio-economic conditions, the possibilities and the needs in the community.
Methods: Primary sources: discussion with community activists, council officers, development workers and businessmen, collection of information on physical resources which could be used by the community, and an administered questionnaire.
General comments: Local people covering all languages were trained as interviewers and were involved in questionnaire drafting.

Report: Chisholm, N. (n.d.) *Economic Profile of Aberfeildy Estate*. London: Community Economy Ltd.
Contact information: Community Economy Ltd (tel. 071 5196447).
Size of study: Area of 972 households, of which a 20 per cent sample was taken.
Aims of study: To assess the potential for community-based economic development.
Methods: Primary sources: discussion with community activists, council officers and development workers; collect information on physical resources which could be used by the community; questionnaire completed by a 20 per cent sample of households.
General comments: Estate is close to Docklands, which has a negative effect upon it, increasing its isolation. Local people were trained to be interviewers. Residents still hoped to find jobs in traditional sectors.

Report: Communicate (1990) *Howden Community Needs Study*. Newcastle Upon Tyne: Communicate.
Contact information: Communicate (tel. 091 2330656).
Size of study: 53 interviews with community groups and individuals, 30 with professionals.

Aims of study: To assess unmet need for community resources among local groups and develop proposals to meet the need.

Methods: Primary sources: questionnaire sent to local groups with core questions followed by in-depth follow-up with individuals and groups for those with special needs

General comments: Funded by Tyne and Wear Development Corporation. Commissioned by Howden Community Forum. There was a strong commitment to involve local people at all stages of the project.

Report: Community Economy Ltd. (1989) *Thorntree Ward Survey*. London: Community Economy Ltd.

Contact information: Community Economy Ltd (tel. 071 5196447).

Aims of study: To find out about the skills, needs and expenditure patterns of the area.

Methods: Primary sources: a two-part questionnaire. (1) A set of picture pages with cartoons and tick boxes looking at skills; (2) a traditional questionnaire, and diary of expenditure for the week. A random sample of 10 per cent of the households in the ward was taken.

Report: Devonshire, M. (1984) *A Short Study of the Neighbourhood Areas of Rhyl and Communities Under Stress*. London: Community Projects Foundation.

Contact information: Community Projects Foundation, 60 Highbury Grove, London N5 2AG.

Aims of study: To examine the pattern of resources, the extent of social needs and the identification of communities under stress.

Methods: Primary sources: a physical mapping exercise, interviews with 85 residents, professional and voluntary groups towards analysis of major issues/services. Secondary sources: analysis of data from other surveys.

Report: Public Participation Consultation and Research (1991) *Ethnic Minority Housing Needs Survey*. London PPCR.

Contact information: Public Participation Consultation and Research (tel. 071 4077462).

Aims of study: To assess the housing needs of ethnic minority communities in Bolton.

Methods: Primary sources: a self-completion questionnaire distributed to respondents and collected by trained staff (the sample was selected using a random interval selection technique).

Report: Shanks, K.B. *et al.* (1990) *Participation: Social Change and Local Action*. London: Community Development Foundation.
Contact information: Community Development Foundation (tel. 071 2265375).
Aims of study: To show how social needs were being met by a variety of local groups and organizations in Thamesmead.
Methods: Interviews with policy makers, local organizations active in social issues and their users, plus a detailed study of four of the organizations. Followed by a survey of local households, considering their problems and awareness/usage of local sources of help.
General comments: Areas of interest: employment and unemployment, health education and training, the environment (both built and natural), transport, women and ethnic minorities.

Profiles by local authorities

Report: Backhouse, R. and Burton, J. (1986) *Taking Books to People – A Practical Community Profile*. London: London Borough of Greenwich.
Contact information: John Lowry, Borough Librarian (tel. 081 8586656).
Aims of study: A profile to assist in the planning and development of an outreach library service.
Methods: Secondary sources: SASPAC as a basis for location planning. Primary sources: contact local community groups, library staff, community workers, local residents and council staff to find out more about needs and resources.

Report: Borough of Sunderland Department of Recreation and Libraries (1985) *An Analysis of the Community Served By Southwick Library*. Sunderland: Sunderland Borough Council.
Contact information: Sunderland Borough Council Department of Recreation and Libraries (tel. 091 5676161).
Aims of study: To use small area census data to assess the library needs of the local population.
Methods: Secondary sources: 1981 small area statistics and SASPAC to produce tables on the library catchment area and the borough as a whole.

Report: Chief Executive (1989) *The Liverpool Quality of Life Survey*. Liverpool: City of Liverpool.
Contact information: Chief Executive's Department, City of Liverpool (tel. 051 2273911).
Size of study: 1840 households (1 per cent sample of the population).
Aims of study: To investigate the level of poverty and affluence in Liverpool.
Methods: Primary sources: 1 per cent sample of Liverpool's population was interviewed and asked which of 22 basic items they could and could not afford.
General comments: Used the same approach as Breadline Britain in 1983.

Report: City of Wakefield MDC (1989) *Knottingley Profile*. Wakefield: City of Wakefield MDC.
Contact information: Jim Kelly or Sally Bigwood (tel. 0924 295151/195169).
Aims of study: To assess if the area is currently benefiting from major council initiatives and contribute to council policy making.
Methods: Secondary sources: collection of information on Knottingley from all council departments. Primary sources: consultation with local residents (numbers involved and methodology not mentioned).

Report: Cleveland County Council Research and Intelligence Unit (1982) *Asian Survey: Education, Housing, Health and Community Provision*. Middlesbrough: Cleveland County Council.
Contact information: Cleveland County Council R&I Unit (tel. 0642 248155).
Aims of study: To consider the social and economic situation of the local Asian community.
Methods: Unknown. Issues considered: education (adults, children), language/literacy, community facilities, health/social services, housing, religion, media.

Report: Cleveland County Council Research and Intelligence Unit (1988) *Pallister Ward: Community Activity and Issues*. Middlesbrough: Cleveland County Council.
Contact information: Cleveland County Council R&I Unit (tel. 0642 248155).

Size of study: 79 interviews.

Aims of study: To enable local communities to identify their own needs and find solutions, while ensuring service agencies are responsive to their problems.

Methods: Primary sources: questionnaires were administered to heads of randomly selected households.

General comments: The number of those interviewed was limited.

Report: Cleveland County Council Research and Intelligence Unit (1989) *Loftus Community Action Area*. Middlesbrough: Cleveland County Council.

Contact information: Cleveland County Council R&I Unit (tel. 0642 248155).

Size of study: 103 interviews.

Aims of study: To identify the needs/perceived assets of area, fieldworkers already deployed, active community/voluntary groups and catalogue facilities for public use/community activity.

Methods: Primary sources: questionnaire-based semi-structured interviews with significant actors, followed by a focused interview to find more subjective areas of interest.

General comments: A very good profile, even though interviews with the general public were not sought.

Report: Cleveland County Council Research and Intelligence Unit (1991) *Citizens' Views on the Performance of their Local Authorities*. Middlesbrough: Cleveland County Council.

Contact information: E.M. Crookston, Cleveland County Council R&I Unit. (tel. 0642 248155).

Size of study: 1727 respondents.

Aims of study: A public attitude survey to gauge satisfaction with council services and identify priorities for service improvements.

Methods: Primary sources: 1727 adults were interviewed following random selection from the electoral register.

Report: Cleveland County Council Research and Intelligence Unit (1991) *Jackson Ward Hartlepool Survey*. Middlesbrough: Cleveland County Council.

Contact information: Cleveland County Council R&I Unit (tel. 0642 248155).

Size of study: 757 participants.

Aims of study: To collect general household information, attitudes to crime, awareness/use of community facilities, needs of children, teenagers and adults for other facilities.

Methods: Primary sources: questionnaires administered in 1:3 households in the ward to interview anyone aged 16 or over who was present.

Report: Colchester Borough Council (1990) *Village Facilities Survey*. Colchester: Colchester Borough Council.

Contact information: Paul Cronk, Colchester Borough Council (tel. 0206 712476).

Aims of study: To list the level of facilities within villages, identify gaps in service provision and the likely impact of future development.

Methods: A questionnaire was sent to all 34 villages in the borough.

General comments: A very comprehensive study.

Report: Crookston, E. and Smith, J. (1990) *The Community and Crime (Hardwick and Whinney Banks)*. Middlesbrough: Cleveland County Council.

Contact information: Cleveland County Council R&I Unit (tel. 0642 248155).

Size of study: 428 interviews completed.

Aims of study: To identify residents' needs and provide baseline data to measure impact of projects.

Methods: Primary sources: a structured interview in the respondent's home (addresses were randomly sampled, and an adult member of the household selected using a grid).

General comments: The survey formed part of an evaluation of the Cleveland Policing of Housing Estates Project.

Report: Eastleigh Borough Council (1992) *Central Eastleigh Community Facilities Survey*. Eastleigh: Eastleigh Borough Council.

Contact information: Carol Newland, Policy/Performance Analyst (tel. 0703 614646).

Aims of study: To establish the demand/supply of community facilities in Eastleigh.

Methods: Secondary sources: demographic assessment and a survey of facilities; not a detailed review of actual demand.

General comments: Rather dry, functional report.

Report: Fife Region and Dunfermline District Councils (1992) *Abbeyview Consultation Paper*. Dunfermline: Fife Region and Dunfermline District Councils
Contact information: Dunfermline District Council (tel. 0383 722711).
Size of study: Abbeyview Estate (13000 people).
Aims of study: To discuss action plan to regenerate Abbeyview, provide better services and enable people to have more influence over decisions affecting their daily lives.
Methods: Primary sources: a community profile based upon the knowledge of local authority employees working in the area and the collection of statistics about Abbeyview; local people were asked to comment upon their findings.

Report: Hamblin, C. (1981) *Pembury: The Library and the Community it Serves*. Maidstone: Kent County Council Education Committee.
Contact information: Pembury Library, Kent (tel. 0892 822278).
Size of study: 71 village residents.
Aims of study: To investigate how far a new library had become part of the community.
Methods: Secondary sources: Kent Household Survey 1968, analysis of library membership cards and distance travelled to use library. Primary sources: a questionnaire administered at the respondent's home. Analysis using SPSS.
General comments: Problems finding up-to-date secondary data, use of electoral register excluded those under 18, survey based on Hillingdon questionnaire. Didn't pilot and later found needed greater adaptation, interviewers untrained, sample not representative ±14 per cent margin of error.

Report: Hereford and Worcester County Council Research and Information Unit (1989) *People Living in Bromsgrove and Redditch District Health Authority Aged 16–64 with Severe Physical Disability*. Worcester: Hereford and Worcester County Council.
Contact information: Hereford and Worcester County Council R&I Unit (tel. 0905 763763).
Size of study: 113 respondents aged 16–64 years.
Aims of study: To survey the needs of people with a severe physical disability and compile a detailed register of people with disabilities.

Methods: Primary sources: face-to-face interviews using a questionnaire adapted from the OPCS questionnaire survey of disabilities and health problems.
General comments: The report largely consists of tables upon which little comment is made.

Report: Hollings, D. (1990) *Farnworth Action Report*. Bolton.
Contact information: Bolton Neighbourhood Economic Development Agency (tel. 0204 22311).
Size of study: 600 personal interviews plus interviews with 40 local employers.
Aims of study: To provide baseline data to help regenerate the area through new jobs, target services and set up local interest groups on identified issues.
Methods: Primary sources: postal questionnaire which identified 300 people willing to take part in follow-up interviews, an additional 300 interviews conducted door-to-door. Forty interviews with local employers using the Employer Labour Market Information questionnaire.

Report: Jennings, A. (1986) *Thorpe Edge Estate Survey*. Bradford: Bradford City Council
Contact information: Bradford Metropolitan Council for Voluntary Service (tel. 0274 722772).
Size of study: 100 respondents.
Aims of study: To assess the most productive use of existing funding in relation to local needs in terms of support group work, neighbourhood community development, neighbourhood advice service or several community services.
Methods: Primary sources: structured interviews with professional community representatives and residents and attendance at public meetings.

Report: Kirkcaldy District Council and Broom III Residents Association (1989) *Broom Survey Report*. Kirkcaldy: Kirkcaldy District Council.
Contact information: Kirkcaldy District Council Department of Housing (tel. 0592 261144).
Size of study: 194 questionnaires issued.
Aims of study: To consult residents about potential improvements

to the area and give them the opportunity to identify previously undetermined issues.

Methods: Primary sources: questionnaire delivered by hand to every house on the estate to be returned to people and locations within the estate (where help could also be provided to complete the questionnaire). The results were analysed manually.

Report: Kneen, P. (1991) *Ragworth Neighbourhood Centre Consultation*. Middlesbrough: Cleveland County Council.
Contact information: Cleveland County Council R&I Unit (tel. 0642 248155).
Size of study: 218 respondents.
Aims of study: To consult estate residents about their views upon the use of a local school as a community centre.
Methods: Primary sources: a short self-completion questionnaire was delivered to every house on the estate.

Report: Lee-Cunin, M. and Ellis, F. (1990) *Support Action Advice – A Community Response to Racial Harassment in the Burley Lodge Area*. Leeds: Leeds City Council.
Contact information: Leeds City Council Health Unit (tel. 0532 474309).
Size of study: Group interviews with 75 people.
Aims of study: To listen to the community response to racial harassment and collate what is said to contribute to a practical approach to tackling racial harassment in the area.
Methods: Primary sources: a short questionnaire distributed to community groups via statutory/voluntary agencies, aiming to reflect the ethnic make-up of the community. Workers associated with groups acted as facilitators and wrote-up outcomes.
General comments: The communities queried what local authorities can do for them.

Report: Merseyside County Council (1983) *The Closure of Smurfit Corrugated Cases Ltd*. Liverpool: Merseyside County Council.
Contact information: Liverpool City Council (tel. 051 2273911).
Aims of study: To report the impact and immediate costs to central and local government of the closure of this medium-sized firm.

Methods: Primary sources: discussion with management/trades unions at the firm. Secondary source: benefits system interpretation by Liverpool Welfare Rights Resource Centre
General comments: A largely statistical study.

Report: Newcastle City Council (1985) *Newcastle Upon Tyne – A Social Audit*. Newcastle: Newcastle City Council.
Contact information: Newcastle City Council (tel. 091 2328520).
Aims of study: To review the effects and hidden costs of government policy upon Newcastle.
Methods: Secondary sources used to compare residents' welfare in 1979 and 1984 using accountancy techniques. Primary sources: a case study approach to examine the qualitative impact on residents' welfare.

Report: Newcastle City Council (1991) *Minority Ethnic Communities Survey 1990*. Newcastle: Newcastle City Council.
Contact information: Research Manager, Newcastle City Council (tel. 091 2328520).
Size of study: 223 residents.
Aims of study: To measure levels of service and satisfaction/dissatisfaction with them.
Methods: Primary sources: a questionnaire was used on respondents chosen through a 1:8 systematic cluster sample of Asian surnames from the electoral register and a non-systematic sample of 11 Afro-Caribbeans in the west of the city.

Report: London Borough of Newham (1985) *Central Newham Social Audit*. London: Newham LBC.
Contact information: London Borough of Newham (tel. 081 4721430).
Aims of study: A public participation exercise to discover social need in Newham and amend local plans accordingly.
Methods: Primary sources: the creation of local working parties to assess local needs and put forward proposals for land/buildings use and the running of local services.

Report: Cheshire County Council Research and Intelligence Unit (1988) *Areas of Family Stress*. Chester: Cheshire County Council.
Contact information: Cheshire County Council R&I Unit (tel. 0244 602424).

Size of study: 1099 individuals plus 238 persons aged 16–24 years.
Aims of study: To profile each area, examine residents' attitudes to their area, their priorities and the impact of neighbourhood centres.
Methods: Primary sources: structured interviews in the home with the householder and other members aged 16–24 years.

Report: Tayside Regional Council Department of Education (1987) *Mid Craigie/Linlathen Area Needs Assessment*. Dundee: Tayside Regional Council.
Contact information: Liz Kay, Senior Community Education Worker (tel. 0382 23281).
Size of study: 356 respondents to household survey.
Aims of study: To discover local views on the use of a community centre and the present needs and 'social' activities of the area.
Methods: A household survey, follow-up interviews with local voluntary and statutory organizations and the collection of secondary data from the census.

Profiles for political purposes

Report: Leeds Liberal Democrat Federation (1991) *The Leeds Housing Survey*. Leeds: Leeds Liberal Democrat Foundation.
Contact information: Leeds Liberal Democrat Foundation (tel. 0532 746052).
Size of study: Questionnaire posted to 11000 households in Leeds City area.
Aims of study: To ascertain residents' priorities with regard to housing problems, what the worst problems are, who suffers from them, the type of homes people prefer and the policy implications of this.
Methods: Questionnaires distributed to streets chosen by party activists.
General comments: The survey was politically motivated, the sampling technique is dubious and there is no clear identification of the response rate.

Report: St John's NUM and Communities Action Committee (1985) *St John's Colliery Maesteg*. Maesteg: St John's NUM and Communities Action Committee
Contact information: Unknown.

Size of study: Town of Maesteg.
Aims of study: To examine the case for and against pit closure. To consider the social/economic effects of closure on the community and assess alternatives to it.
Methods: Secondary sources used to assess the quantifiable costs to the community compared with savings made by the National Coal Board and to study the social consequences.
General comments: It is a campaigning document. Its conclusions rest on the assumption that unemployment remains high.

Self-study profiles

Report: Down Ampney Village Appraisal Group (1991) *A Village Appraisal: Down Ampney, Gloucestershire*. Gloucester.
Contact information: Ros Leigh, Gloucester Rural Community Council Fieldworker (tel. 0285 713152).
Size of study: 136 respondents.
Aims of study: Village consultation about new developments and contribute to Cotswold District Council's structure plan.
Methods: Questionnaire delivered personally by members of the steering group and collected later; all residents aged 11 + were consulted. Analysis completed using a computer.
General comments: Very well presented and interesting village appraisal.

Report: Maybank Community Association (1984) *The Second Maybank Project Report*. Maybank: Maybank Community Association.
Contact information: Unknown.
Size of study: 147 respondents.
Aims of study: To examine the needs of the area and make recommendations to local and central government.
Methods: Secondary sources used to collect demographic information. Primary sources: questionnaire to discover residents' attitudes to key local issues. Make recommendations to local and central government. Complete follow-up study within 5 years. This was achieved via a study of 20 per cent of the households in the area and public meetings.

Report: Mid Craigie and Linlathen Community Forum (1992) *Mid Craigie and Linlathen Community Plan*. Dundee: Mid Craigie and Linlathen Community Forum.

Contact information: Nigel Glynn, Team Leader, Community Education Office, St Vincents Community Wing, Glenn Connor Drive, Dundee DD4 8EP.

Aims of study: To develop a community plan originating from local people taking responsibility for their area and working together to rebuild their community.

Methods: Establishment of a group of local activists (members of the community) to push forward consultation plans for the area.

Report: Safe Estates for Women (1992) *Bloomsbury Safety Audit Phase One*. Birmingham. Safe Estates for Women.

Contact information: Safe Estates for Women, c/o Heartlands Community Trust, Waterlinks House, Richard Street, Heartlands, Birmingham B7 4AA.

Size of study: The Bloomsbury Estate.

Aims of study: To highlight women's safety and the importance and means of involving women in the decision-making process.

Methods: Primary sources: a 'planning for real' exercise, production of videos highlighting the problems on the estate, a walk around the estate with local officials.

Report: Safe Estates for Women (1992) *Bloomsbury Safety Audit Phase Two*. Birmingham: Safe Estates for Women.

Contact information: Safe Estates for Women, c/o Heartlands Community Trust, Waterlinks House, Richard Street, Heartlands, Birmingham B7 4AA.

Size of study: The Bloomsbury Estate (191 respondents).

Aims of study: To enable women on the estate to express their views and experience of unsafe features on the estate and use the report to press for improvements which will promote safety.

Methods: Primary sources: define a relevant definition of safety; map out problem spots on the estate; discussions with local community groups, the community architect, police, housing department and fire brigade to set the survey objective; choose representative sample of women who live, work or regularly visit the estate; priority search questionnaire administered door to door by women residents and analysed by Priority Search Team in Sheffield.

Profiles by universities, polytechnics and colleges

Report: Ahmed, T. (1990) *Beeston Voices a Social Audit*. Leeds: Leeds Urban Audit.
Contact information: Policy Research Unit, Leeds Metropolitan University (tel. 0532 832600).
Aims of study: A social audit focusing on people's needs and the resources provided to meet them.
Methods: Secondary sources: information from official statistics. Primary sources: in-depth semi-structured interviews with professionals working in Beeston and questionnaire distributed to local groups via community workers.

Report: Bowen, J. *et al.* (1983) *What Suits Shipley?* Leeds: Leeds Metropolitan University.
Contact information: Judith Bowen, Leeds Metropolitan University (tel. 0532 832600).
Size of study: 885 respondents.
Aims of study: To assess the library needs of people using Shipley town centre.
Methods: Primary sources: street interviews using structured questionnaires at random sites in the town. Manual analysis. Secondary sources: census data for Bradford MBC and wards close to Shipley town centre.

Report: Bradford Youth Research Team (1988) *Young People in Bradford*. Bradford: Bradford and Ilkley Community College.
Contact information: Department of Applied and Community Studies, Bradford and Ilkley Community College (tel. 0274 753111).
Size of study: 300 + interviews.
Aims of study: To gather information on the working, family and social lives of young people in Bradford.
Methods: Primary sources: a questionnaire was sent to a 1 per cent sample of young people of Bradford taken from the careers service data.

Report: Brady, S. and Hughes, G. (1991) *Seacroft Sounds Out: A Community Profile*. Leeds: Policy Research Unit.
Contact information: Policy Research Unit, Leeds Metropolitan University (tel. 0532 832600).

Aims of study: A community profile to assess the effectiveness of targeted resources.
Methods: Secondary sources collected and a local social history compiled. Primary sources: distribution of a self-completion questionnaire to all adult residents, semi-structured group interviews with residents and also with key professional workers.

Report: Brady, S. *et al.* (1990) *Skills in the Community*. Leeds: Policy Research Unit.
Contact information: Policy Research Unit, Leeds Metropolitan University (tel. 0532 832600).
Aims of study: A detailed examination of local labour supply characteristics in two areas of high unemployment.
Methods: Primary sources: a large postal survey, follow-up interviews with a smaller selected sub-sample of residents and local meetings to which respondents could bring queries.

Report: Bretton Hall College (1984) *Walton Parish Council Local Study 1984*. Walton: Walton Parish Council.
Contact information: Bretton Hall College (tel. 0924 830261).
Size of study: Village of Walton (population unknown).
Aims of study: To study resident's views on the state of their community, the role of their parish council and their hopes for Walton's future, providing a baseline for policy planning.
Methods: Primary sources: students used semi-structured interviews to investigate the history of Walton, recreation pursuits of 5–11 and 16–20 year olds and parish councillors; a questionnaire administered to local households. Analysis and presentation by College.

Report: Browne, L. (1989) *Church and the Community*. Leeds: Policy Research Unit.
Contact information: Policy Research Unit, Leeds Metropolitan University (tel. 0532 832600).
Aims of study: To identify community needs, resources of the church and how the church can use its resources to respond to community needs.
Methods: Secondary sources: census and local authority. Primary sources: qualitative data from interviews with people who live and work in the area and church members. A questionnaire given to people using church facilities and an assessment of church resources.

Report: Donaldson, L.J. and Odell, A. (n.d.) *Aspects of the Health and Social Services Needs of Elderly Asians in Leicester – A Community Survey*. Leicester: University of Leicester.
Contact information: Department of Community Health, University of Leicester, Leicester Royal Infirmary (tel. 0533 541414).
Size of study: 857 respondents.
Aims of study: Descriptive study to provide information which is not routinely available; to assist in service planning and generate hypotheses for further study.
Methods: Interviews with people aged 65 and over from ethnic minorities in Leicester. Areas covered: demography, family/social contact, lifestyle, physical capacity, language/communication, knowledge/use of social services.

Report: Hill, M. (1991) *The Walker Riverside Study*. Newcastle: University of Newcastle.
Contact information: Department of Social Policy, University of Newcastle (tel. 091 2226000).
Size of study: Survey of 500 households.
Aims of study: To respond to local residents' concerns about youth crime and gather information to stimulate interest/organization among residents.
Methods: Secondary sources: collection of local statistical data. Primary sources: semi-structured interviews with councillors, community leaders and professionals, group interviews with community organizations/projects and at street level with young people; social survey of 500 households and feedback to focus on priorities with local people.
General comments: Rush to get project done to meet council and LDC deadlines and meetings. Initially, not too much consultation with local people leading to problems of ownership. Trained local people as interviewers. Sample from electoral register response poor due to void properties and failure to answer front door. Local political culture will not support community action unless it is channelled through council structures.

Report: Hudson, R. *et al.* (1984) *Undermining Easington – Who will Pay the Price of Pit Closures?*. Durham: Durham University, Department of Geography.
Contact information: Department of Geography, Durham University (tel. 091 3742865).

Aims of study: To investigate the social effects of coal mining job losses in Easington district.

Methods: Statistical and quantitative analysis of social effects (using multipliers). Qualitative analysis of the impact on individuals, families and communities and the meaning of pit closures to Easington's residents (using interviews and questionnaires).

General comments: Taken from Geddes, M. (1988) *Social Audits and Social Accounting: An Annotated Bibliography and Commentary*. London: South Bank Polytechnic.

Report: Percy-Smith, J. and Sanderson, I. (1991) *Needs in Leeds*. Leeds: Policy Research Unit.

Contact information: Policy Research Unit, Leeds Metropolitan University (tel. 0532 832600).

Aims of study: To pilot a model of needs auditing generating new information through both top-down and bottom-up methods of enquiry.

Methods: Secondary sources: data collected to provide indicators of needs. Primary sources: a 10 per cent postal needs survey of adult residents, in-depth interviews with a sub-sample to collect more qualitative information, structured discussions with community representatives and public meetings to bring all the above together.

General comments: Good explanation of theoretical background and discussion of methods.

Report: Roberts, H. (1991) *Accident Prevention: Child Protection – A Community Approach*. Glasgow: University of Glasgow

Contact information: Ms Helen Roberts (tel. 041 3393118).

Aims of study: To identify factors predisposing children to be at risk of, or protected from, accidents.

Methods: Primary sources: using group interviews, a local household survey and case studies to expose strategies used by parents to maintain child safety in a demonstrably unsafe environment.

Other profiles

Report: Gloucester County Council (1990) *A Comparison of Collegiate Board Areas in Gloucester*. Gloucester: Gloucestershire County Council.

Size of study: Area of study, Gloucester County.

Aims of study: To collate social economic information from 1981 census with reference to the collegiate board areas for comparison with national statistics.

Methods: Secondary sources: 1981 census and the Annual Residential Land Availability Report by the County Planning Department.

General comments: No public consultation; information from the 1981 census was nine years out of date. No references.

Index